# History Matters

## A Student Guide to
## U.S. History Online

# History Matters

## A Student Guide to
## U.S. History Online

Alan Gevinson
Kelly Schrum
Roy Rosenzweig

George Mason University

Bedford/St. Martin's

Boston ◆ New York

**For Bedford/St. Martin's**

*Executive Editor for History:* Mary Dougherty
*Director of Development for History:* Jane Knetzger
*Developmental Editor:* Bryce Sady
*Production Editor:* Kendra LeFleur
*Senior Production Supervisor:* Joe Ford
*Senior Marketing Manager:* Jenna Bookin Barry
*Production Assistants:* Kristen Merrill, Anne True
*Copyeditor:* Patricia Herbst
*Text Design:* Gretchen Toles for Anna Palchik Design
*Cover Design:* Donna Lee Dennison
*Composition:* Karla Goethe, Orchard Wind Graphics
*Printing and Binding:* Haddon Craftsman, Inc., an R. R. Donnelley & Sons Company

*President:* Joan E. Feinberg
*Editorial Director:* Denise B. Wydra
*Director of Marketing:* Karen Melton Soeltz
*Director of Editing, Design, and Production:* Marcia Cohen
*Managing Editor:* Elizabeth M. Schaaf

Library of Congress Control Number: 2004107880

Manufactured in the United States of America.

9  8  7  6  5  4
f  e  d  c  b  a

*For information, write:* Bedford/St. Martin's, 75 Arlington Street, Boston, MA 02116
(617-319-4000)

ISBN: 0–312–45000–1
EAN: 978–0–312–45000–7

# Preface

In 1996 when the Center for History and New Media and the American Social History Project first began to develop the idea for the website *History Matters: The U.S. Survey Course on the Web* (http://historymatters.gmu.edu), the web was a very different place than it is today. Coverage of many historical topics was sparse at best; a search on an icon of American history like Franklin Delano Roosevelt might yield fewer than 100 hits in a search engine. Today the same search gives you more than 150,000 hits. There are now literally tens of millions of historical documents available online. Secondary sources are less abundant, but the Internet offers some stunning collections.

The very abundance of the web's offerings, however, has proved unsettling. Students and teachers continually ask: How do I find the "good stuff?" How do I avoid misleading and even fraudulent documents? This book (plus the website on which it is based) provides one answer to those questions by offering a safe path through the overwhelming and sometimes confusing maze of historical sources and interpretations that we encounter on the web and by providing an annotated guide to the very best websites available for the study of American history.

As a guide to history on the web, this book differs from similar books in two main ways. First, we take a *selective approach;* rather than providing a catalog of the thousands of sites available, we focus on the most illuminating and comprehensive resources. Second, we see this book as a starting point for further student investigation. We particularly emphasize collections of primary sources that allow students to engage in historical research on their own, and we provide guidance on how to locate, evaluate, and cite those resources. The most important way for students to become intelligent consumers of historical resources online is by becoming good historians and applying the tools of critical analysis that historians have always used to evaluate and understand their sources.

## Content and Organization

This volume contains an introduction for students, descriptions of 250 of the best websites available for the study of U.S. history, a subject index, a primary source index, a glossary, and an appendix on search engines. With an introduction to doing history research online, we explain the crucial difference between primary and secondary sources, offer some tips on critically evaluating history websites, and provide guidance on how to analyze the primary sources that are now available online in such profusion. Many teachers worry that plagiarism is more common with online historical work, but students who follow our advice on plagiarism and our rules for the proper citation of online sources will avoid that danger.

We devote most of the book to the 250 carefully vetted and annotated sites, the best from the *History Matters* website. We chose sites not only for the quantity of resources they include but also because they reflect the breadth of the American experience with particular attention to the lives of ordinary people and not just the rich and powerful. We have placed the annotations in nine conventional chronological divisions to reflect how most students study U.S. history. Two indexes — by topic and by type of source — help locate relevant sites from those alternative vantage points. For those new to the Internet as a whole, we provide a glossary of common technical terms and an overview of web search engines.

## Teaching with *History Matters*

Our book offers the basis for using the web to create innovative and engaging assignments for the undergraduate survey of American history or even research seminars in history organized around online primary sources. Our website, *History Matters,* offers a number of these assignments under "Digital Blackboard." Some exercises focus on developing skills of document analysis, and on how to read a source carefully and closely for its historical evidence. For example, Sue Luftschein and David Jaffee ask students to work in pairs to analyze images from the Metropolitan Museum of Art website. Another type of digital history assignment asks students to create a historical presentation using online sources. Here, the public nature of the web as a medium helps to give greater relevance and interest to the assignment than is often the case with typical history papers. Jen Fraser of San Mateo Middle College High School asks students to create an online magazine that covers aspects of culture, politics, arts, music, and lifestyles from the 1920s. These kinds of assignments make students producers rather than mere consumers of historical information. Of course, many teachers using this book may want to devise their own assignments. Just as the web is still young, so are web-based teaching approaches. The most inventive are yet to be devised.

## Acknowledgments

The website *History Matters: The U.S. Survey Course on the Web,* is a collaborative project developed by the American Social History Project/Center for Media and Learning (ASHP/CML) at the Graduate Center, City University of New York, and the Center for History and New Media (CHNM) at George Mason University. The group that initially developed the project included Pennee Bender, Steve Brier, Joshua Brown, and Roy Rosenzweig. They were later joined by Ellen Noonan and Kelly Schrum. We want to thank our colleagues on the *History Matters* team and also our funders — the National Endowment for the Humanities, the Kellogg Foundation, the Rockefeller Foundation, George Mason University, the Virginia Foundation for the Humanities, City University of New York, and the New York Council for the Humanities.

The 250 website annotations in this book were specifically selected and edited for this volume by Alan Gevinson and Kelly Schrum, but they are based on the much larger number of annotations written for the website over a period of many years by Laura Beveridge, Megan Elias, Alan Gevinson, Katharina Hering, Michael Laine, Wendi Manuel-Scott, Michael O'Malley, Ellen Pearson, Elena Razlogova, Roy Rosenzweig, Kelly Schrum, and John Summers. Additional thanks go to the graduate research assistants at George Mason University who helped with the research and preparation of the manuscript: Jeremy Boggs, Rustin Crandall, James Halabuk, Katharina Hering, Stephanie Hurter, and Amanda Shuman. We also want to express our appreciation to Joan Feinberg, Elizabeth Schaaf, Patricia A. Rossi, Bryce Sady, and Kendra LeFleur of Bedford/St. Martin's, who helped envision and shape this book.

Roy Rosenzweig

# Contents

Preface    *v*


## 1. An Introduction to History Research Online    *1*

Distinguishing between Primary and Secondary Sources    *2*
Evaluating U.S. History Websites    *6*
Analyzing Primary Sources    *13*
A Word about Plagiarism    *17*
Citing Online Sources    *20*
Using This Guide    *21*


## 2. A Selection of Top U.S. History Websites    *27*

**General Websites for U.S. History Research**    *27*
**U.S. History Websites by Time Period**    *43*

Three Worlds Meet and Colonization, Beginnings to 1763    *43*
Revolution and the New Nation, 1754–1820s    *47*
Expansion and Reform, 1801–1861    *54*
Civil War and Reconstruction, 1850–1877    *65*
Development of the Industrial United States, 1870–1900    *70*
Emergence of Modern America, 1890–1930    *85*
Great Depression and World War II, 1929–1945    *105*
Postwar United States, 1945 to the Early 1970s    *116*
Contemporary United States, 1968 to the Present    *124*


Appendix: Using Search Engines Effectively    *135*

A Glossary of Common Internet Terms    *139*

Primary Source Index    *143*

Subject Index    *145*

# History Matters

A Student Guide to
U.S. History Online

# 1

## An Introduction to History Research Online

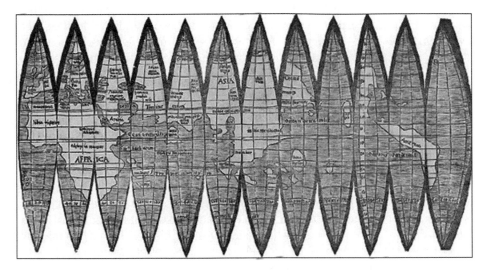

The Waldseemuller Global Gores Map (1507).
*(James Ford Bell Library, University of Minnesota)*

It is the first meeting of your U.S. history class and as you read through the upcoming assignments, you begin to do a little research. Or it is the night before your first research paper is due and you frantically look for resources you can access before sunrise. Perhaps the assignment requires you to compare European perspectives of the New World with those of American Indians. Or to discuss challenges that African Americans faced in the nineteenth century. Maybe you were asked to discuss how women's lives changed in the first half of the twentieth century and how these changes relate to larger themes in U.S. history.

If you start your pursuit of historical resources for these assignments on the Internet, you will not be alone. In a recent study, college students reported heavy use of the Internet for research. Almost 75 percent use it more frequently than they use traditional resources.[1]

Searching for materials about European explorers or American Indians, you might visit websites with fifteenth- or sixteenth-century maps (see above), tales of contact, or archaeological findings. To study the experiences of African Americans in the United States before and after the Civil War, you could visit websites on slavery, abolition, legal history, and popular culture. To investigate political activism and changing roles of women, you could view a collection from the National Woman Suffrage Association or do research on Margaret Sanger or Emma Goldman. You could read Zora Neale Hurston's first story to learn about the Harlem Renaissance from a female perspective. Or you could study advertisements to analyze the rise of a highly gendered consumer market. While searching for sources, though, you might inadvertently end up on a website about Indian motorcycles, the home page for the rock band Slaves on Dope, or a website advertising "Pick Up Magic" — all of which appear among the first results of Google (http://www.google.com) searches on "Indian," "slaves," and "women." If you add "history" or "American history" to these searches, or more specific information, such as "African American history," the results are better but still require careful sifting and evaluation.

The Internet has become a vast, rich, and primarily free library offering a wealth of materials for researching U.S. history. Thousands of websites offer analysis, documents, images, music, and film, although not all offer high-quality resources and information. If you visit Yahoo (http://www.yahoo.com), you will find a directory of almost 8,000 U.S. history websites. A Google search on "colonial American history" yields nearly 1 million results, including syllabi, textbooks, and hotels located close to historic sites. How do you wade through this enormous and sometimes confusing online library to find reliable, high-quality sources of information? How can you avoid advertisements or personal pages created by history enthusiasts whose standards of historical analysis may not meet those of your teacher? Being web savvy does not automatically translate into critical use of online resources.

This book is designed to make the process easier and faster. You might start by finding out what kinds of information are available online and when a visit to the library will be more useful. If the Internet offers what you are seeking, sharpen your skills for evaluating websites and assessing whether a particular website presents accurate information and reliable U.S. history resources. The section "Analyzing Primary Sources" (see page 13) offers strategies and guidelines to help you think critically about historical evidence. When you are ready to take notes, read "A Word about Plagiarism" (page 17) to boost your awareness of this important topic, and then read "Citing Online Sources" (page 20) so that you are sure to correctly cite the websites that you use for your assignments and research papers.

While you are considering the many different types of websites and the kinds of materials they offer, one helpful strategy for selecting the most revelant resource is to think about the categories of primary and secondary sources that historians use to identify both traditional and online materials.

## Distinguishing between Primary and Secondary Sources

Both primary and secondary sources are valuable for learning about U.S. history, but they serve different purposes and provide different kinds of information (see table). Primary sources are pieces of the past, surviving records and evidence that historians use to analyze historical events and themes. These

## Primary versus Secondary Sources

| Primary Sources | Secondary Sources |
| --- | --- |
| A photograph | An article on photographic journalism in a history journal |
| A diary | A book written by a leading historian about nineteenth-century women's diaries |
| The Constitution | A recording of a lecture on the Constitution |
| An advertisement | An article in *Smithsonian* about advertisements for appliances in the 1940s |
| A 1950s Coke bottle or a contemporary Coke can | A website about Coca-Cola advertisements |
| A musical recording | A web log about jazz |
| A Portuguese map of America drawn in 1580 | A modern map showing sixteenth-century Portuguese colonies |
| Ticker tape from 1929 | A chart of 1920s economic indicators in a textbook |

include official records, speeches by political leaders, diaries and letters by ordinary Americans, census data, novels, newspaper articles, sermons, photographs, paintings, advertisements, and material culture, such as pottery fragments or a can of shaving cream. Secondary sources are writings by historians, journalists, and others who generally use primary sources to interpret the past. They provide analysis, interpretation, and summary, placing questions and evidence in a historical context and explaining their significance. Secondary sources invariably reflect the author's point of view as the author shapes historical material, both primary and secondary sources, into an interpretation of the past.

Primary sources are the building blocks of history. They require you to be the historian, investigating the past, interpreting materials, and trying to make sense out of the historical record. Primary sources are often incomplete, but they are invaluable because they offer an exciting opportunity to engage directly with thoughts, ideas, and materials from a particular time period or with a specific historical issue. They illustrate how complex the past can be, challenging you to grapple with uncertainties and to create your own historical arguments. They allow you to develop a convincing argument on historical questions such as whether or not the United States should have dropped atomic bombs on Japan. Historians seek to do more than just express their opinions on such questions. They use documents, such as military records, newspaper articles, or diaries by President Harry S. Truman, his advisers, and Japanese leaders, some of which can be found at the *Truman Presidential Museum and Library* website [222]* to build arguments about the past rooted in historical research.

Here is an example to illustrate how different secondary sources might approach primary evidence. Scholars who study the rise of consumer culture in the twentieth century disagree about the relationship between cause and effect. Have advertisers shaped the desires and purchasing habits of consumers? Or have consumers controlled the market while advertisers struggled to follow popular trends?

Michael Schudson, a communications professor who specializes in American media and advertising, argues that advertising does not coerce consumers into buying products. He writes in his book *Advertising, The Uneasy Persuasion* that "advertising is much less powerful than advertisers and critics of advertising claim, and advertising agencies are stabbing in the dark much more than they are practicing precision microsurgery on the public consciousness."[2]

In contrast, Susan Strasser, a history professor who writes about American consumer culture, opens her book *Satisfaction Guaranteed* — on the creation of an American mass market — with the story of Crisco, a new product introduced by Procter & Gamble in 1912. To exert greater influence in the cottonseed oil market, Procter & Gamble "attempted to design consumer demand to meet the needs of production and company growth." The company successfully "made Crisco in order to sell it." Strasser argues that Proctor & Gamble did not respond to consumer need or demand. They invented a product and through a host of new marketing strategies — grocery promotions, direct mail, free recipe books, recipe contests, and free samples — created a market.[3]

These authors present consumer culture and the role of advertising in American life in different ways. They provide examples based on primary sources and develop their analyses to support larger arguments about historical change and cause and effect, but they reach different conclusions. In the following quotation from a U.S. history textbook (a secondary source), a description of the rising twentieth-century consumer culture provides a much broader overview and credits both advertising and consumers as active forces:

> Mass production of a broad range of new products — automobiles, radios, refrigerators, electric irons, washing machines — produced a consumer goods revolution. In this new era of abundance, more people than ever conceived of the American dream in terms of the things they could acquire. . . . The advertising industry linked the possession of material goods to the fulfillment of every spiritual and emotional need. Americans increasingly defined their social status, and indeed their personal worth, in terms of material possessions.[4]

The textbook avoids controversy, stating both that the advertising industry "linked" possessions with needs and that consumers "defined their social status" through consumer goods.

---

*Numbers in brackets refer to websites annotated in Ch. 2, A Selection of Top U.S. History Websites.

Because one primary source alone is not enough to help you answer broad questions about the relationship between consumer demand and market pressure, looking at a range of advertisements can be an excellent way to begin researching these questions. Take, for example, a relevant primary source, a 1923 advertisement in *Good Housekeeping* magazine for Listerine mouthwash (Fig. 1). The text reads, "What secret is your mirror holding back? . . . She *was* a beautiful girl and talented, too. . . . Yet in the one pursuit that stands foremost in the mind of every girl and woman — marriage — she was a failure." This advertisement shows how advertisers attempted to influence consumption and exemplifies several common marketing strategies. It provides an example of advertisements that promoted guilt and feelings of inadequacy. This young woman's failures were the result not of lack of beauty or skill but of lack of hygiene and inappropriate consumer choices. Depending on your research question, the next step might be to examine Listerine ads in other publications or in the following year or to compare this ad with advertisements for other products in the same magazine.[5]

The Internet offers a wealth of primary and secondary sources for understanding the past. The most important thing to keep in mind is what kind of source you are encountering when you go to a website. Many websites offer either primary materials or secondary interpretations; other websites offer both. For example, the more than 150 websites in the Library of Congress's *American Memory* [4] project are online archives of primary sources. They include limited contextual material, such as background or interpretive essays, because their central purpose is to offer free access to more than 8 million primary sources that can help scholars and students engage with the past and develop their own historical interpretations.

By contrast, online exhibits organized by history teachers, museums, or historical societies often put more emphasis on secondary analysis. They

Fig. 1 A 1923 advertisement for Listerine. *(Good Housekeeping)*

have a particular story to tell, and they organize relevant primary sources to tell it. For example, the Smithsonian Institution's National Museum of American History website *A More Perfect Union* provides an overall narrative of the forced internment of 120,000 Japanese Americans living on the West Coast during World War II. Yet unlike most books on the internment, the exhibit also presents primary sources, including music, personal accounts, artifacts, and images. This website provides a secondary narrative as well as an online archive.[6]

Like textbooks and history books, websites presenting secondary sources, such as explanatory essays or guides, have a point of view. They select certain sources or evidence to address a theme or argue a point. When the point of view is not strongly expressed or reflects widely held views, this bias may not be obvious. Another Smithsonian website, *George Washington: A National Treasure,* presents the first president favorably — a view that most Americans share. But one reviewer of the website writes that it views Washington in an uncritical manner that is more befitting a monarch than a president.[7]

In other cases, the interpretation presented on a website is more controversial. One example is *The Alger Hiss Story: Search for the Truth,* created by author and journalist Jeff Kisseloff. In the 1930s, Whittaker Chambers, a former Communist, accused Alger Hiss, a former State Department official, of providing the Soviet Union with secret documents. Hiss was convicted of perjury and sentenced to five years in prison. This highly publicized case fueled McCarthyism and spread fear of communism. Hiss's guilt was a highly contested issue, and it is still debated by historians today. Kisseloff, however, clearly states his belief in Hiss's innocence as well as his goal of creating the website to present the "full facts" of Hiss's life. The secondary source material, in the form of essays, provides layers of analysis supplemented by brief trial excerpts, newspaper clippings, and news footage. This website offers an interesting introduction to the case. But because not all historians share Kisseloff's viewpoint, additional research would be required to analyze Alger Hiss in historical perspective.[8]

Some websites present highly controversial viewpoints that are shared by few, if any, serious historians. For example, you can find websites created by people who deny that the Holocaust occurred — a position that no credible historian embraces. The following advice on evaluating websites offers strategies for finding reliable U.S. history sources on the web.

## Evaluating U.S. History Websites

Although the Internet offers many valuable secondary sources — whether in the form of museum exhibits that interpret a historical topic, an essay by a well-informed Civil War enthusiast, or a scholarly article on a subscription-based website such as *History Cooperative* [19] or *JSTOR* [19] — the library is often a better starting point for secondary sources than the web. Good scholarship aims to present a balanced perspective and to be clear about motives and goals. Historical scholarship in print has been reviewed by academics, publishing institutions, and librarians. Your college library — unlike the web — has thousands of interpretive works selected by librarians and publishers. One of the Internet's great advantages is the free exchange of opinion and information that can take place. But this freedom can become a disadvantage because there are no safeguards to screen for quality, honesty, and academic rigor. This situation places special responsibility on you, the user.

Where the web excels is in providing primary sources. Even major research libraries cannot offer the wealth of primary sources readily available online. Many websites serve as online archives, providing hundreds, even thousands, of primary materials for historical analysis.

There are some basic things to look for when you visit a U.S. history website. The first is the author. Who created the website? Who wrote, gathered, or posted the materials presented? Sometimes authorship is straightforward, as you can see in this screenshot from the Library of Congress's American Memory collection *The African-American Experience in Ohio, 1850–1920* (Fig. 2). This website prominently displays its affiliation with the Library of Congress as well as with the Ohio Historical Society, the organization that provided the materials for digitization. "American Memory" identifies the website as part of a rich body of digital primary source materials relating to the history and

**Fig. 2** Screenshot from *The African-American Experience in Ohio, 1850–1920* [133]. *(Library of Congress)*

culture of the United States, including the papers of George Washington [53] and Abraham Lincoln [65], Civil War photographs [99], African American sheet music [134], early motion pictures [154], and music and stories collected from many parts of the country [193, 198, 201, 203]. On other websites, the author is difficult or even impossible to identify, which may indicate an effort to deceive or mislead the user.[9]

Information concerning a website's author or creator is particularly important when the website presents historical interpretation. A good researcher tries to determine the author's point of view and then evaluates how that perspective might affect the presentation of sources. For example, conservative and liberal scholars are likely to view the presidencies of Richard Nixon or William Clinton from different perspectives, just as an Israeli and a Palestinian would probably interpret the history of the Middle East in different ways. Point of view can even affect online collections of primary sources: Someone strongly committed to one interpretation of the past might select primary sources that largely support that position.

A related question is who hosts or publishes a website. Sometimes an "about," "credit," or "background" page offers information on who created or sponsors a website and why. An email address or contact information may provide clues as well. Knowing the affiliation of a website's author can help you determine the reputability of a source. Where is the author, webmaster, or main contact located? Is he or she affiliated with a museum, library, or college?

If no useful identifying information is readily apparent, you can try shortening the URL (Uniform Resource Locator). Start by removing the last characters, stopping before each forward slash (/), and pressing "Enter" to see where the new URL takes you. If you receive an error page, remove another section of the URL. Sometimes this process takes you to a larger subheading within a project. For example, material located at **http://www.gwu.edu/~nsarchiv/NSAEBB/NSAEBB103/index.htm** offers documentation of the efforts of President John F. Kennedy, shortly before his assassination, to establish a dialogue with Cuban president Fidel Castro. The materials are presented by the *National Security Archive* [242], a nongovernmental institution that publishes declassified government materials. If you remove "index.htm," you find yourself on the same page. Removing the next section of the URL leaves you with **http://www.gwu.edu/~nsarchiv/NSAEBB**, a webpage that presents a list of all "Electronic Briefing Books" offered by the *National Security Archive*. Truncating once more to **http://www.gwu.edu/~nsarchiv** leads to the project's home page, where you can click on the "about" link to learn more about the website's creator, host, and purpose:

> The National Security Archive is an independent non-governmental research institute and library located at The George Washington University in Washington, D.C. The Archive collects and publishes declassified documents acquired through the Freedom of Information Act (FOIA).[10]

Not all URLs work this way. To present vast quantities of material, website creators increasingly use databases to organize their data. This structure has many advantages, often making it easier to search the full text of documents and to access specific evidence, but it can sometimes result in URLs that are very long and may not be permanent. In some cases, unwieldy URLs make it difficult to cite and share valuable resources. For example, this URL appears when you read *The Ballot and the Bullet*, a publication compiled by Carrie Chapman Catt in 1897 to challenge the claim that women should not be allowed to vote because they did not serve in the military:

> http://memory.loc.gov/cgi-bin/query/r?ammem/naw:@field+(SOURCE +@band(rbnawsa+n2415)):@@@$REF$

The URL is long and complicated. To share the resource or locate the book at a later date, you may need to reference the main web page that offers this material, *Votes for Women: Selections from the National American Woman Suffrage Association Collection, 1848–1921* (http://memory.loc.gov/ammem/naw/ nawshome.html) [176], and browse or search by title (*The Ballot and the Bullet)* or author (*Carrie Chapman Catt*).

In contrast, the *Avalon Project* [7], a collection of more than 3,500 full-text documents in law, history, economics, politics, diplomacy, and government, offers static web pages, pages not generated by a database, with permanent URLs. For example, you can read the Mutual Defense Treaty between the United States and the Republic of Korea (1953) at http://www.yale.edu/lawweb/ avalon/diplomacy/korea/kor001.htm. This structure also offers advantages and disadvantages. It generally means that the full text of the documents is not searchable, as it would be with a database. The URL in this case, however, offers information about the creator as well as the location of the document within the project under the headings "diplomacy" and "korea."

Shortening the URL to http://www.yale.edu/lawweb/avalon/diplomacy/ korea or to http://www.yale.edu/lawweb/avalon/diplomacy does not reveal anything about the website's creator, but shortening a bit more takes you to the main page of the *Avalon Project:* http://www.yale.edu/lawweb/avalon. If you shorten again, you find the Yale University School of Law, the website's sponsor. If you remove "lawweb," you reach the Yale University home page.

Yale University and its School of Law are well-respected institutions that lend credibility to the *Avalon Project* and the material it provides. Not every URL that ends in "yale.edu," however, is officially sanctioned by Yale University. Students and faculty often have access to URLs that include an institutional name. So http://www.ucla.edu/~jones might be the URL for someone named Jones who is affiliated with University of California at Los Angeles, but it is not necessarily run as an official university website. *The Alger Hiss Story: Search for the Truth* is a good example. The URL, http://homepages.nyu.edu/~th15, identifies New York University as the host server. If you truncate the URL to http://homepages.nyu.edu, though, you find the following, strongly worded disclaimer: "Welcome to the home of the personal pages of faculty, staff, and students of NYU. These pages do not in any way constitute official New York University content. The views and opinions expressed in the pages are strictly those of the page authors, and comments on the contents of those pages should be directed to the page authors."

To identify personal pages hosted on large institutional servers, you can look for personal names, a tilde (~), or words such as "home," "user," or "people." Commercial servers, such as AOL, Yahoo, and Geocities, also host many personal websites. On these servers, there are no definite rules regarding author and content quality. Some personal pages provide valuable historical resources, and websites designed or hosted by large institutions sometimes offer flawed or incomplete information. A good researcher approaches all websites with skepticism and asks questions about why this material is available and who funded and created the website. Here are two general rules: Museums, libraries, and colleges create websites to present historical resources for educational purposes. Individuals often create personal websites to share their passion for a certain topic, and they may or may not offer credible content.

When evaluating websites, consider the domain name. The Domain Name System (DNS) allows websites to use names that stand for a website's numeric address, which is known as an Internet Protocol (IP) address. Two-letter codes, such as *.uk* and *.jp*, are usually country codes, signifying a country or territory such as the United Kingdom or Japan. Many websites, especially in the United States, end in three-letter codes. Some of the most common are

.com    unrestricted but intended for commercial use

.edu    restricted to U.S. educational institutions

.gov    restricted to U.S. government

.mil    restricted to U.S. military

.net    unrestricted but intended for network providers

.org    unrestricted but intended for organizations that do not fit in other categories

The domain name is not a definitive indicator of quality, but it can provide you with an important clue about the author and purpose of a website to use when evaluating its resources — especially if you are planning to use materials or analysis from that website for a history paper or project. Start by asking yourself if the domain name seems appropriate for the content. URLs that end in *.edu* come from educational institutions. As previously noted, personal pages can also end with *.edu*, but in general *.edu* websites are created by teachers, librarians, and scholars for educational purposes. For example, the rich resources available through Duke University's Digital Scriptorium [147, 160, 180] or the University of California, Berkeley, Digital Library [148, 155] include *.edu* in their web addresses. Similarly, URLs with *.gov* are created by government agencies, giving them credibility. *American Memory* [4] URLs include *.gov,* as do resources found in the *Archival Research Catalog* at the National Archives and Records Administration [6].

Many commercial websites (*.com*), in contrast, are designed to sell products or establish brand identity, such as **http://www.pepsi.com** or **http://www**

.nike.com. Other commercial websites provide information and services, such as http://www.united.com or http://www.landsend.com. In general, commercial websites are not designed to provide academic materials, but some websites in the .com domain offer a wealth of historical resources, such as *Anti-Imperialism in the United States, 1898–1935* [139] (http://www.boondocksnet.com/ai), created by independent scholar Jim Zwick. This website contains 800 essays, speeches, pamphlets, political platforms, editorial cartoons, petitions, and pieces of literature on American imperialism and its opponents. Another example is the *Freedmen's Bureau Online* [94] (http://www.freedmensbureau.com), created by Christine's Genealogy Websites, which provides an extensive collection of Freedmen's Bureau records and reports, including more than 100 transcriptions of reports on murders, riots, and labor contracts.

Information about when a website was created or updated can also be a valuable indicator of a website's reliability, although an archive of primary sources need not be updated frequently to remain useful. The website *Indian Affairs: Laws and Treaties* [25], created by the Oklahoma University Library between 1996 and 2000, offers the digitized contents of a seven-volume collection of treaties, laws, and executive orders relating to United States–Indian affairs. There is no need to update this website regularly because it provides a fixed set of historical materials. As long as the primary sources are available and the links work, this website will remain valuable.

Websites that provide links to online resources, however, do require regular updating. For example, the Kingwood College Library hosts a website named *American Cultural History, 1960–1969*. Created by reference librarians, the website offers links to websites and primary sources related to major events, individuals, and cultural developments of the 1960s. Brief essays help contextualize specific trends in art, film, books, fashion, and music, but there are many dead links to websites that are no longer functional. A useful concept and once a valuable resource, in its present state this website might not be the best place to find high-quality materials quickly.[11]

The content of a website can also be very revealing. What is the purpose of the website? Does it present facts or opinions? Does it have a particular bias or point of view? A biased website can provide useful information, but a site is most valuable when it clearly identifies its goals and distinguishes between fact and opinion. Is there a clear presentation or selection of materials? Is the website trying to sell something? More than 100 websites sponsored by or affiliated with the Public Broadcasting Service (PBS) cover topics in U.S. history, ranging from medicine in early America to Tupperware to Jimmy Carter's presidency. Many of these websites are created to promote PBS videos and offer little of historical significance beyond a description of the videos, a timeline, and classroom discussion questions. *The American Experience: Hawaii's Last Queen* is a good example, offering only these basics plus a quiz and a bibliography.[12]

Roughly twenty PBS websites, however, offer a wealth of primary sources and tools for historical analysis. *Africans in America* [1], for example, created as a companion to the series of the same name, traces the history of Africans in

America from the fifteenth-century slave trade to the Civil War. The website offers 245 primary documents, including images and maps. Knowing that an online resource is hosted or created by PBS enhances credibility, but that affiliation alone does not provide enough information about the depth and content of the website. Further investigation is needed to determine if the material offered is valuable for historical research.[13]

A related question is "Who is the intended audience for this particular website?" Some PBS websites are created to provide teachers with information on videos. Others are created for students as well as teachers to promote historical research. Asking about the audience might provide insight into whether a website is appropriate for your project. The *Philip Morris Advertising Archive*, created by Philip Morris Incorporated, provides a good example. Created as part of the Master Settlement Agreement with the tobacco industry, this website offers more than 55,000 color images of tobacco advertisements, dating back to 1909. It is part of a larger online resource that offers more than 26 million pages of documents on the research, manufacturing, marketing, and sale of cigarettes from four tobacco companies and two industry organizations. The website presents an unparalleled amount of materials for researching tobacco and cigarettes in American life, yet it is frustrating to use because the search engine is confusing and results are difficult to understand. The settlement agreement mandated that companies make this information available, but did not require a user-friendly format.[14]

You might also ask what kinds of resources a website offers. Perhaps it offers secondary sources, such as a summary or an analysis of various questions in American history. One example is the encyclopedic description of the Boston Tea Party available at the *North Park University Web Chronology*:

> On December 16, 1773, American patriots dressed as Mohawk Indians boarded the vessels of the East Indian Company docked in the Boston harbor and dumped all the tea that was on the three ships into the ocean. They emptied 342 chests of tea which was valued at more than 10,000 pounds. This event became known as the "Boston Tea Party."

Other websites offer primary sources relating to the well-known event, such as the first-person account of the Boston Massacre by Boston shoemaker George Robert Twelves Hewes, available on the website *History Matters: The U.S. Survey Course on the Web* [21].[15]

If a website offers primary materials, are they complete or edited? Are sources well documented? Spelling or grammatical errors should raise concerns about reliability. Similarly, broken links to other websites may suggest that a website has not been updated recently. Links to unreliable or similarly biased websites may raise questions about an author's credibility or motives.

Considering all of these factors will help provide you with a good sense of the quality of a website and the materials it presents. One additional way to assess the reliability of a website is to investigate whether other websites and organizations find it valuable. Run a "link check" with Google by typing "link:"

followed by the complete URL into the Google search field, as follows (see the appendix, "Using Search Engines Effectively," for more tips):

link: **http://etext.virginia.edu/salem/witchcraft**

This link check on *Salem Witch Trials: Documentary Archive and Transcription Project* [45], created by University of Virginia religious studies professor Benjamin Ray, returns 332 results. This means that more than 300 websites link directly to this archive. The fact that many of the links come from library, teaching, and university websites indicates that an academic audience has favorably reviewed these materials.

You can also look for reviews of a website in web or print publications that research and evaluate websites for educational use, such as the MERLOT *Project* **(http://www.merlot.org)**, the *Scout Report* **(http://scout.wisc.edu)**, and the website *History Matters* [21].[16]

## Analyzing Primary Sources

Once you find primary sources, what do you do with them? The Internet opens the door to resources, especially primary materials, formerly unavailable to most college students — such as Thomas Jefferson's personal letters, a handwritten diary kept by Martha Ballard, an eighteenth-century midwife, and film footage depicting everyday life in the early twentieth century. You can study maps presenting data on every presidential election from 1860 to 1996 or look at characteristics of civil rights volunteers. Using new kinds of primary sources to understand the past can be challenging, however. Reading a letter from the eighteenth century is very different from reading a nineteenth-century diary or a twenty-first-century email message. Analyzing early films requires different skills than interpreting a map. When historians write textbooks and other history books, they sift through large collections of materials to select relevant items. Scholars present materials from a particular point of view after considering related historical events and trends and analyzing relevant primary and secondary sources. Analyzing primary sources is exciting and rewarding, but it requires careful attention to details, language, and historical context.[17]

The first step is to consider the kind of primary source you are using. What is unique about that source? Who created it? When was it created and how? What did it mean for the creator at the time? What original value did it possess? How did its value change over time? The questions depend on the nature of the source. The website *History Matters* [21] contains guides to "making sense" of different kinds of evidence. In guides such as *Making Sense of Maps* and *Making Sense of Films*, and in a series of interviews, such as *Analyzing Blues Songs* or *Analyzing Abolitionist Speeches*, scholars suggest questions to ask when you are working with primary sources as different as political cartoons and quantitative data.[18]

According to oral historian and scholar Linda Shopes, for example, questions such as "Who is talking?" and "Who is the interviewer?" are crucial when you are reading an oral history interview. The answers provide insight into the circumstances that created the interview as well as into the recorded words. Interviewers shape the dynamic of an interview, asking certain questions and responding differently to various kinds of information. The individual being interviewed assesses the interviewer, deciding what he or she can say and what is best left unsaid. For example, a grandparent being interviewed by a grandchild for a family history project may suppress unpleasant memories to protect the child or preserve family myths.[19]

When you are studying American popular song, historian Ronald G. Walters and musicologist John Spitzer point out, there are important issues to investigate in addition to asking who wrote and performed the song. What did the song mean when it was created? Did it mean different things to different audiences? What does it mean now? What can songs tell us about people and society? Musicians and their audiences are social actors. While they reflect the world around them, they also interpret and change it. For every anti–Vietnam War song such as the "I-Feel-Like-I'm-Fixin'-To-Die Rag" (1967), there were pro-war (or anti-anti war) songs such as the "Ballad of the Green Berets" (1966). Songs such as these are most valuable for telling us what concerned people, how they interpreted various issues, and how they expressed hopes, ideals, and emotions.[20]

An early-nineteenth-century inventory of a house demonstrates what you can learn by asking specific questions about resources. In an interview available on the website *History Matters*, historian and museum curator Barbara Clark Smith analyzes an inventory that lists the belongings, including slaves, of a man named Thomas Springer. After Springer's death in 1804, the court in New Castle County, Delaware, appointed appraisers to assess and record the value of his belongings (Fig. 3). Smith shows how the document offers valuable information about daily life, values, and household goods in this time period, providing insight into the life of someone who was not famous and left few historical artifacts. What did Thomas Springer own? What can his possessions tell us about his life? What can we learn about the lives of others in his household, such as his wife and two African American men?[21]

This inventory begins with the clothing of the deceased, including coats, shirts, trousers, and boots. The dollar amount placed on various items provides a sense of what they might have cost. Springer's clothing, worth $30 in 1804, was more valuable than his "feather Bed, Bedding and Bedstead," valued at $26. The inventory reveals some family behavior and patterns. The teacups and tea table suggest participation in the ceremony of tea. "Two spinning wheels" hints at the work done by women in the Springer household.

Among the inventoried items are "one negro man, named Abe: 9 years to serve, valued at 180.00" and "one old negro man, a slave 66 years old, named Will . . . 00.00." Their presence on the list reveals several important things about the period and the status of slaves. In some respects, this is routine — these men are listed as possessions alongside clocks and trousers. But it is also interesting to note that only one is listed as a slave. In Delaware in 1804, slavery was

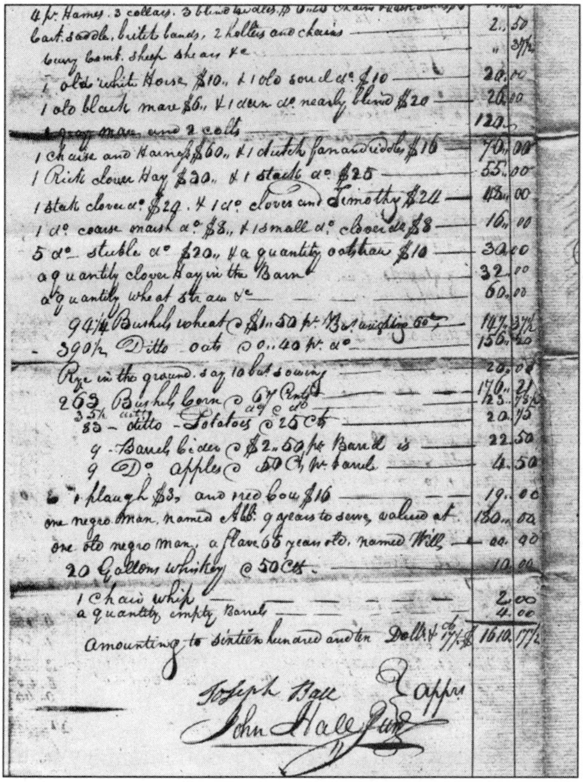

**Fig. 3** An inventory of the belongings of Thomas Springer after his death in 1804. The value of Springer's possessions informs research into the economic and cultural conditions of his time. Of particular interest are "one negro man, named Abe [?]: 9 years to serve, valued at 180.00" and "one old negro man, a slave, 66 years old, named Will ... 00.00." What story do the age and appraisal of these two men tell us?
*(National Museum of American History)*

ending, primarily because it was less profitable in the North than in the South. The "negro man, named Abe" had "9 years to serve." This wording suggests that Abe may have negotiated his freedom for exchange for a certain number of years of service, as some African Americans did after the American Revolution. At the end of the set period, Abe would have received his freedom and possibly a small amount of money. Will, in contrast, is described as a slave, and no monetary value is placed on him, probably because of his age.

With strategies for analyzing the inventory, we can learn about daily life, economics, social relationships, and work from this one document. The inventory can become even more valuable when compared with similar lists from Springer's town or county and with those from neighboring areas. Examining inventories over a period of ten years would reveal what different people owned, which items were typical, and which things were extraordinary. With a large enough pool of inventories, you could start to count the items listed and utilize quantitative analysis to study trends.

Reading an inventory may seem a relatively straightforward task, but vast amounts of information are likely to be hiding beneath the surface. Similarly, it is easy to look at a photograph and mistakenly think of it as a reproduction of reality, a historical mirror. In *Making Sense of Documentary Photography*, historian James Curtis discusses how visual evidence requires different tools of analysis. Scholars ask who wrote a letter or autobiography and why. It is equally important to ask who took a photograph and why was it taken. Who sponsored it? What was the photographer's goal or intent in making the image? How was the photograph taken, and how was it presented to the public? Important stories hidden within images can teach us many things about the past.[22]

Documentary photography emerged in the second half of the nineteenth century and was initially considered journalism rather than art. Documentary photographers were seen as event recorders, and they often encouraged this misconception, presenting themselves as fact gatherers and denying political or social motives. It is impossible, though, even with a goal of recording events, to avoid shaping a picture. As photographers create an image, they make many decisions about subject, angle, framing, what to include, and, equally important, what to exclude. Printing, selecting, editing, and presentation shape the final product, and all of these decisions are influenced by the photographer's goals, as well as by mechanical limitations.

During the Civil War, as Curtis writes, bulky equipment and long exposure times meant that photographers could not capture combatants in action. Instead, they took pictures of battlefield remains, sometimes rearranging scenes for dramatic effect. After the bloody Battle of Gettysburg in 1863, photographer Alexander Gardner had a dead soldier moved across a field and placed in a rocky corner. The resulting photograph, *Rebel Sharpshooter in Devil's Den* (Fig. 4) remains a powerful image of the Civil War despite knowledge of the photographer's intervention.[23]

Manipulation of subjects remains an important tool for documentary photographers. This becomes apparent from looking at companion photographs. Documentary photographers often take a series of pictures to ensure backup images. The process also provides opportunities to later select images that best convey their sense of the scene or reflect the meaning they want to present. Photographers working for the Farm Security Administration (FSA) during the

**Fig. 4** *Rebel Sharpshooter in Devil's Den*, a photograph of a body posed by Civil War photographer Alexander Gardner. *(Library of Congress)*

Great Depression were required to submit all of their negatives from an assignment, creating an amazing record of companion photographs that detail the
steps involved in obtaining a desired image. A collection of these photographs
is available at the Library of Congress website *America from the Great
Depression to World War II: Photographs from the FSA-OWI, 1935–1945* [183].[24]

One of the most enduring images of the Great Depression, known as
*Migrant Mother*, depicts a woman and her children in a California migrant labor
camp (Fig. 5). This is the last in a series of six photographs that FSA photographer Dorothea Lange took on a rainy afternoon in March 1936. The composition
of this image, however, was not accidental. Lange crafted the photograph carefully, changing perspective, changing camera angles, excluding details and people, and rearranging poses. The six images demonstrate Lange's control of the
scene and of the actions of her subjects. In her initial frame, Lange showed
thirty-four-year-old Florence Thompson and four of her children. In the second
frame, the oldest of the four is outside the tent. Thompson had seven children,
but Lange, hoping to elicit sympathy from her middle-class audience, concen-
trated on the youngest ones. The trunk and empty pie tin in the foreground of
the fifth photograph attest to the family's itinerancy and struggle for survival,
but they do not appear in the final, now famous, frame. For the sixth photograph, Lange posed the two young girls with their heads resting on their
mother's shoulders. She turned their faces away from the camera and brought
Thompson's right hand to her face, a strategy for framing the face and drawing
attention to the subject's feelings. This final picture, as Lange intended, became
a symbol of both the suffering occasioned by the Great Depression and human
dignity. The five companion images, however, show that *Migrant Mother* is not
a simple document or a reflection of reality. The image and its message were
shaped by Lange, her purpose, her sponsor, and her audience.[25]

Learning various strategies to analyze historical evidence creates new
opportunities and introduces new questions. When you think carefully about
the kinds of materials you are using and what they tell you that other resources
cannot, your research question will become more refined, and you may be led
to unexpected conclusions. Start by asking general questions, move to specific
questions relevant for your source, and then explore how the primary source
fits into a broader context.

## A Word about Plagiarism

Plagiarism did not come into existence with the Internet — printed materials
have long provided ready content for copying. But the Internet, and the mixture
of skill and naiveté with which many approach it, creates new opportunities as
well as potential dangers. Online texts, images, sounds, and videos are easy to
copy, paste, and manipulate. This may seem to make note taking easier, but it
also makes plagiarism — intentional or unintentional — as easy as clicking on
"copy" and "paste." Many college students are not aware of the full meaning of
plagiarism and its repercussions. College policies vary, but students who are

**Fig. 5** From documentary to icon of the Great Depression, Dorothea Lange's *Migrant Mother* is an example of subject manipulation.
*(Library of Congress)*

caught plagiarizing can receive anything from a failing grade in a course to expulsion. Plagiarism does not have to be deliberate to be wrong; unintentional plagiarism is subject to the same penalties.[26]

Plagiarism is presenting the words, work, or opinions of someone else as if they were your own without proper acknowledgment. Plagiarism also occurs if you borrow someone else's sequence of ideas, arrangement of material, or pattern of thought and do not acknowledge the source. If your history paper gives the impression that you are the author of words, ideas, or conclusions that are in fact the product of another person's work, you are guilty of plagiarism. This is equally true for published and unpublished materials (such as a paper written by another student) as well as for any material found on the Internet. Someone else's words are someone else's words, whether printed or electronic, published or unpublished.

How can you avoid plagiarism? Here are some steps you can take:

1. Learn about plagiarism, paraphrasing, and college regulations by visiting your college writing center or library. For additional definitions, suggestions, and resources, visit the websites listed below.

2. Take notes carefully, especially when taking notes from a website to a computer or when typing notes directly into a computer from a book. If you copy and paste, *always* enclose the entire text in quotation marks, and include a full citation to the source. If you paraphrase, make sure you understand the original text and then set it aside. Write the ideas in your own words, and be sure to cite the author as the source of the ideas even though you are not quoting directly.

3. When you quote directly from a source to a computer document (including all citation information), change the color of the quotation with your word processor to make it stand out from the rest of the text. The color will serve as a visual reminder that something is a quotation and requires proper citation.

4. Update your list of sources, both primary and secondary, as you take notes and work on drafts. See "Citing Online Resources" (page 20).

5. Keep a copy of each source you use, including photocopies of print articles and key passages from books. Print copies of online sources or email yourself copies. Store the copies together.

6. As you research and write, save drafts of your work. When you begin to make revisions, create a new copy and save the original, so that you create a record of your work and the development of your thoughts.

Studying other people's ideas and reading primary sources are central to conducting historical research. Historians use quotations from primary sources to illustrate their arguments, and they include quotations from other scholars to place their own discussion in a broader context. Both of these are acceptable, and indeed desirable, aspects of writing a history paper. The key to avoiding plagiarism is to always credit the source of direct quotations, paraphrased information, and other people's ideas and to use your skills to create your own original ideas and historical analysis.

■ *Additional Online Resources on Research, Plagiarism, and Documenting Sources*

*St. Martin's Handbook,* Andrea Lunsford
    **http://bedfordstmartins.com/smhandbook**

*Research and Documentation Online,* Diana Hacker
    **http://dianahacker.com/resdoc**

*Writer's Handbook,* University of Wisconsin–Madison, Writing Center
    **http://www.wisc.edu/writing/Handbook**

*Documenting Sources,* George Mason University Writing Center
    **http://www.gmu.edu/departments/writingcenter/handouts/docu.html**

## Citing Online Sources

The best strategy for avoiding unintentional plagiarism is to take notes carefully and keep a thorough record of all sources. Citing sources is a key part of conducting historical research, and it provides an important record of your research process. To keep a "running" bibliography as you begin your research, create a separate list of complete citation information — in addition to the source information and specific page numbers or URLs that you include in your notes. If you compile this list, then at a glance you can assess the sources you are using, evaluate the balance of primary and secondary materials, and decide if you need to seek out new kinds of sources to gain a well-rounded perspective on an issue.

The bibliography for a history course may vary slightly from bibliographies or reference lists required in other courses. Your teacher might provide specific guidelines for citing various kinds of sources. Standards for citing electronic resources began to emerge in the past decade. The guidelines listed here provide a good model for citing websites and other electronic resources in history writing. They are based on *The Chicago Manual of Style,* 15th edition.[27]

■ *Computer Software*
List the name of the software, the version used, the publisher, and the location of the publisher. Do not separate the version from the name of the software.

U.S. History: The American West CD-ROM Ver. Windows NT, Fogware
    Publishing, San Jose, CA.

■ *Website*
List the author or organization that is responsible for the site, followed by the website title in quotation marks. Give the URL and then, in parentheses, the date on which you accessed the website.

Hooker, Richard. "The Idea of America," http://www.wsu.edu:8000/~dee/
    AMERICA (accessed January 14, 2003).

■  *Email Message*

Ask permission from an author before citing his or her email message. List the author of the email, the subject header, and the date on which it was sent. If the email is personal, note that but do not include the author's email address.

> Temple, Lynn. "Re: Question about the Bedford flag." Personal email message, March 26, 2003.

■  *Listserv Message*

The format is similar to that of an email message, but you should include the email address of the listserv.

> Dyke, Liz Ten. "South Asians in 19th century USA." Listserv message, January 17, 2003, h-world@h-net.msu.edu.

■  *Newsgroup Message*

This format is similar to that of a listserv message, but you should include the location of the newsgroup.

> Rosa, Domenico. "Vietnam's Women of War." Newsgroup message, January 19, 2003, soc.history.war.Vietnam.

■  *Material from an Information Service or Database*

List the service, agency, or corporation responsible for collecting or presenting the information such as the author, the name of the article (if applicable) in quotation marks, the name of the database (if applicable) italicized or underlined, followed by any website reference.

> United Nations Population Division, "World Population Prospects: The 2000 Revision," United Nations Population Information Network, http://www.un.org/popin.

## Using This Guide

Online resources for learning about U.S. history are opening an exciting world of primary materials and analysis to college students everywhere. To take full advantage of these opportunities, learn to find and evaluate reliable websites, beginning with those listed in this guide. Then start to think about strategies for critically analyzing the range of online sources you can access, asking questions specific to the kinds of sources you are using.

The collection of 250 websites included in this book is not definitive. It is intended as a useful guide to finding valuable online resources for exploring the American past. The authors of this book reviewed more than 5,000 websites to select this list with the goal of illustrating the strengths of the Internet for learning about the past and the incredible range of resources and perspectives available, from images of the Atlantic slave trade [37] through oral histories with activists involved in the 1999 World Trade Organization protests in Seattle,

Washington [250]. Many excellent websites were not included, but those we have chosen represent some of the best materials available for use in a U.S. history course.

Most of the websites presented here are available at no cost. Increasingly, however, publishers are creating significant historical databases and making them available for a fee. If colleges and universities subscribe to these databases, the materials become available for student use. Fees range widely and can be quite high, but some of these websites offer large quantities of materials otherwise unavailable, such as historical newspapers and periodicals. *ProQuest Historical Newspapers* [33] allows access to the *New York Times* (1851–2001), the *Washington Post* (1877–1988), the *Wall Street Journal* (1889–1986), and the *Christian Science Monitor* (1908–1991). *Accessible Archives* [66] provides close to 200,000 articles from nineteenth-century newspapers, magazines, and books, including *Godey's Lady's Book* (1830–1880), one of the most popular nineteenth-century publications, and the *Pennsylvania Gazette* (1728–1800). *HarpWeek* [95] presents full-text images and transcriptions from *Harper's Weekly* (1857–1912). Given the size and scope of these resources, some subscription websites are included in this guide. Their status is clearly identified in the description, and the symbol for subscription websites $\boxed{\$\$}$ is included. Ask your librarian if your school subscribes to these resources, and how you can access them.

Additional symbols indicate the kinds of resources available on each website. $\boxed{\text{圖}}$ signifies that there are significant textual materials, such as books, documents, letters, or diaries. $\boxed{\text{❐}}$ indicates photographs, paintings, or drawings. $\boxed{\text{◀ᴺ}}$ means that audio files, usually music, speeches, or oral history interviews, are available. $\boxed{\text{🎞}}$ means that the website offers film or video clips, ranging from early film footage to contemporary commercials and interviews.

The first section of this list, "General Websites for U.S. History Research," introduces resources covering broad periods of time. Some of these are general, such as *Hypertext on American History from the Colonial Period until Modern Times* [24], created by a history professor in the Netherlands. Others deal with a specific topic or kind of resource across centuries, such as *Women and Social Movements in the United States, 1775–2000* [36], created by history professors Thomas Dublin and Kathryn Kish Sklar, or *American Time Capsule: Three Centuries of Broadsides and Printed Ephemera* [5], from the Library of Congress's American Memory collection.

The second section, "U.S. History Websites by Time Period," lists websites that provide materials on topics and time periods covered in U.S. history survey courses, including American Indian life and European exploration, the creation of the U.S. Constitution, industrialization, the Civil War, Vietnam, and AIDS. We organized this section into nine common chronological groupings:

Three Worlds Meet and Colonization, Beginnings to 1763

Revolution and the New Nation, 1754–1820s

Expansion and Reform, 1801–1861

Civil War and Reconstruction, 1850–1877

Development of the Industrial United States, 1870–1900

Emergence of Modern America, 1890–1930

Great Depression and World War II, 1929–1945

Postwar United States, 1945 to the Early 1970s

Contemporary United States, 1968 to the Present

Finally, we provide an appendix on performing effective Internet searches as well as a glossary of common Internet terms to assist you in learning about electronic resources. In addition, the indexes can be a valuable starting point if you are looking for specific resources. The primary source index lists websites by the kind of primary sources available, including Advertising, Maps, Music, and Speeches. The subject index is organized by topic, including African Americans, International Relations, and Women as well as more specific listings and individual names, such as Architecture, Mark Twain, and World War I.

Whatever your assignment or interests, you are sure to find valuable resources awaiting exploration. The Internet can help you track down answers to historical questions or explore unique primary sources to challenge traditional explanations in American history. If you use it wisely, the Internet can be a valuable tool for learning about the past.

Kelly Schrum

# NOTES

[1]Pew Internet Project, "The Internet Goes to College: How Students Are Living in the Future with Today's Technology" (September 15, 2002), http://www.pewinternet.org/reports/toc.asp?Report=71 (accessed October 3, 2003).

[2]Michael Schudson, *Advertising, The Uneasy Persuasion: Its Dubious Impact on American Society* (New York: Basic Books, 1996), xiii.

[3]Susan Strasser, *Satisfaction Guaranteed: The Making of the American Mass Market* (Washington, D.C.: Smithsonian Institution Press, 1989), 3–28.

[4]James L. Roark et al., *The American Promise: A History of the United States,* 3rd ed. (Boston: Bedford/St. Martin's, 2005), pp. 836–37.

[5]*Good Housekeeping,* July 1923, p. 175.

[6]National Museum of American History, "A More Perfect Union," http://americanhistory.si.edu/perfectunion/experience (accessed October 3, 2003).

[7]Smithsonian National Portrait Gallery, "George Washington: A National Treasure," http://www.georgewashington.si.edu/portrait (accessed October 3, 2003).

[8]Jeff Kisseloff, "The Alger Hiss Story: Search for the Truth," http://homepages.nyu.edu/~th15 (accessed October 12, 2003).

[9]American Memory, Library of Congress, "The African-American Experience in Ohio, 1850–1920," http://memory.loc.gov/ammem/award97/ohshtml/aaeohome.html (accessed October 15, 2003).

[10]Thomas S. Blanton, "National Security Archive," http://www.gwu.edu/~nsarchiv/nsa/the_archive.html (accessed January 10, 2004).

[11]Kingwood College Library, *American Cultural History, 1960–1969,* http://kclibrary.nhmccd.edu/decade60.html (accessed October 30, 2003).

[12]PBS, *American Experience: Hawaii's Last Queen,* http://www.pbs.org/wgbh/amex/hawaii (accessed October 3, 2003).

[13]PBS, *Africans in America,* http://www.pbs.org/wgbh/aia (accessed October 3, 2003).

[14]Philip Morris Incorporated, *Philip Morris Advertising Archive,* http://www.pmadarchive.com (accessed October 15, 2003). See also *Tobacco Archives,* http://www.tobaccoarchives.com.

[15]North Park University, *United States of America Chronology,* http://campus.northpark.edu/history/WebChron/USA/TeaParty.html (accessed October 15, 2003); Center for History and New Media and American Social History Project, *History Matters,* "George Hewes' Recollection of the Boston Massacre," http://historymatters.gmu.edu/d/5825/ (accessed October 15, 2003).

[16]*Merlot Project* (Multimedia Educational Resource for Learning and Online Teaching), http://www.merlot.org (accessed October 15, 2003); Internet Scout Project, University of Wisconsin–Madison, *Scout Report,* http://scout.wisc.edu (accessed October 15, 2003); CHNM and ASHP, *History Matters,* http://historymatters.gmu.edu (accessed October 15, 2003).

[17]American Memory, Library of Congress, *Thomas Jefferson Papers,* http://memory.loc.gov/ammem/mtjhtml/mtjhome.html; Film Study Center, Harvard University, and CHNM, *Do History,* http://dohistory.org; American Memory, Library of Congress, *America at Work, America at Leisure: Motion Pictures from 1894 to 1915,* http://memory.loc.gov/ammem/awlhtml/workleisSubjects02.html; Geospatial and Statistical Data Center, University of Virginia Library, *U.S. Presidential Election Maps: 1860–1996,* http://fisher.lib.virginia.edu/collections/stats/elections/maps/1864.gif; University of Wisconsin-Madison, *Online Data Archive,* http://dpls.dacc.wisc.edu/archive_txt.htm.

[18]*Making Sense of Evidence* guides (*Making Sense of Documents*) and interviews (*Scholars in Action*) available at CHNM and ASHP, History Matters, http://historymatters.gmu.edu/browse/makesense.

[19]See Linda Shopes, *Making Sense of Oral History,* http://historymatters.gmu.edu/mse/oral.

[20]See Ronald G. Walters and John Spitzer, *Making Sense of American Popular Song,* http://historymatters.gmu.edu/mse/Songs.

[21]See Barbara Clark Smith, *Analyzing an 1804 Inventory,* http://historymatters.gmu.edu/mse/sia/inventory.htm.

[22]See James Curtis, *Making Sense of Documentary Photography,* http://historymatters.gmu.edu/mse/Photos.

[23]American Memory, Library of Congress, *Rebel Sharpshooter in Devil's Den* (or *The Home of a Rebel Sharpshooter, Gettysburg*), http://memory.loc.gov/ammem/cwphtml/cwphome.html (accessed October 15, 2003).

[24]American Memory, Library of Congress, *America from the Great Depression to World War II: Photographs from the FSA-OWI, 1935–1945,* http://memory.loc.gov/ammem/fsowhome.html.

[25]For more on the *Migrant Mother* photograph, see *What Can Companion Images Tell Us?* http://historymatters.gmu.edu/mse/Photos/question4.html.

[26]Johns Hopkins University History Department guidelines; Diana Hacker, *The Bedford Handbook for Writers,* 4th ed. (New York: St. Martin's, 1994), 477–479; *Straight Talk about Plagiarism from Bedford/St. Martin's,* bedfordstmartins.com/plagiarism/flyer.

[27]*The Chicago Manual of Style,* 15th ed. (Chicago: University of Chicago Press, 2003). Citation information cited in Jules R. Benjamin, *A Student's Guide to History,* 9th ed. (Boston: Bedford/St. Martin's, 2004), 138–141. For more information on citing resources for history papers, see pp. 127–151.

# 2

# A Selection of Top U.S. History Websites

Photograph of Company E, 4th U.S. Colored Infantry, c. 1864, at *Africans in America* [1].
*(Library of Congress)*

## GENERAL WEBSITES
## FOR U.S. HISTORY RESEARCH

### 1. Africans in America
*PBS Online*
http://www.pbs.org/wgbh/aia

This well-produced website, created as a companion to the PBS series of the same name, traces the history of Africans in America up to Reconstruction in four chronological parts. The website provides 245 documents, images, and maps linked to a narrative essay. *The Terrible Transformation* (1450–1750) deals with the beginning of the slave trade and slavery's growth. *Revolution* (1750–1805) discusses the justifications for slavery in the new nation. *Brotherly Love* (1791–1831) traces the development of the abolition movement. *Judgment Day* (1831–1865) describes debates over slavery, strengthening of sectionalism, and the Civil War. In addition to the documents, images, maps, and essays (approximately 1,500 words per section), the website presents 153 brief descriptions by historians on specific questions in the history of slavery, abolition, and war in America. Although the website lacks a search engine, it remains a valuable introduction to the study of African American history through the Civil War.

27

## 2. Alexander Street Press
http://www.alexanderst.com

This subscription website offers seventeen separate databases of digitized materials that provide either firsthand accounts (diaries, letters, and memoirs) or literary efforts (poetry, drama, and fiction). Twelve databases pertain to American history and culture. *Early Encounters in North America: Peoples, Cultures, and the Environment* offers primary sources documenting cultural interactions from 1534 to 1850. *The American Civil War: Letters and Diaries* draws on more than 400 sources and supplies a day-by-day chronology with links to documents. *Black Thought and Culture* furnishes monographs, speeches, essays, articles, and interviews. *North American Immigrant Letters, Diaries, and Oral Histories* covers 1840 to the present. *North American Women's Letters and Diaries: Colonial to 1950* provides full-text letters and diaries from more than 1,000 women — totaling more than 21,000 documents and approximately 120,000 pages — written between 1675 and 1950. Five databases present American literary writings: *Latino Literature: Poetry, Drama, and Fiction*; *Black Drama*; *Asian American Drama*; *North American Women's Drama*; and *American Film Scripts Online*. In addition, *Oral History Online* provides a reference work with links to texts, audio, and video files. While the databases include previously published documents, many also contain thousands of pages of unpublished material. In addition to keyword searching, the databases provide "semantic indexing" — extensive categorical search capabilities. For more specific information, see *Women and Social Movements in the United States, 1775–2000* [36].

## 3. AMDOCS: Documents for the Study of American History
*Anschutz Library, University of Kansas*
http://www.ukans.edu/carrie/docs/amdocs_index.html

This website provides links to more than 440 documents, most of which are related to the nation's political, diplomatic, military, and legal history. Arranged chronologically, the website begins with excerpts from Christopher Columbus's journal of 1492 and ends, at present, with President George W. Bush's May 1, 2003, address announcing the end of major combat operations in Iraq. Materials include speeches, statutes, treaties, court decisions, memoirs, diaries, letters, published books, and a few songs. The website offers easy access to canonical documents in American history.

## 4. American Memory: Historical Collections for the National Digital Library
*Library of Congress, American Memory*
http://lcweb2.loc.gov/amhome.html

This expansive archive of American history and culture features more than 8 million items from 1490 to the twentieth century. Currently this website includes material from 120 collections, some from libraries and archives around the world. Strengths include the early American Republic, with documents and papers on the Continental Congress, U.S. Congress, early Virginia religious petitions, George Washington, and Thomas Jefferson; the Civil War, including Abraham Lincoln's papers and Mathew Brady photographs; and exploration and settlement of the West. Collections offer papers of inventors, such as Alexander Graham Bell, Emile Berliner, Samuel F. B. Morse, and the Wright Brothers, and composers, such as Leonard Bernstein and

Aaron Copland. The website also features New Deal–era documentation projects, such as Farm Security Administration photographs, Federal Writers' Project life histories, the Historic American Buildings Survey, and "Man on the Street" interviews following the Pearl Harbor attack. Entertainment history is amply represented with collections on the American Variety Stage, Federal Theatre Project, early cinema, and early sound recordings. African American history, ethnic history, women's history, folk music, sheet music, maps, and photography also are well documented. Digitized images from materials not included in specific *American Memory* websites may be searched using the Library of Congress's *Prints and Photographs Catalog* (**http://lcweb.loc.gov/rr/print/catalog.html**), where users can browse fifty-two topical groups of images or search the Library's holdings.

### 5. American Time Capsule: Three Centuries of Broadsides and Printed Ephemera
*Library of Congress, American Memory*
**http://memory.loc.gov/ammem/rbpehtml/pehome.html**

This website furnishes more than 10,000 items of ephemera — "transitory documents created for a specific purpose, and intended to be thrown away." Items dating from the seventeenth century to the present are from the United States and London, although the majority comes from the nineteenth century. Materials include posters, advertisements, leaflets, propaganda, and business cards, and relate to subjects such as the American Revolution, slavery, western migration, the Civil War, the Industrial Revolution, travel, labor, education, health, and woman's suffrage. Users can search by keyword or browse by author, title, genre, or printing location. There is a special presentation on popular types of broadsides and ephemera.

### 6. Archival Research Catalog (ARC)
*National Archives and Records Administration (NARA)*
**http://www.archives.gov/research_room/arc**

In addition to providing a catalog for those planning to visit NARA, *ARC* offers approximately 124,000 digital images of governmental textual records, photographs, and maps. Materials date from the Colonial period to the recent past. *ARC* includes items on presidents, the nation's wars, slavery, civil rights, and American Indians. Approximately 500 images date from the seventeenth and eighteenth centuries. The search engine is clearly organized and invites queries on specific historical materials or general themes. To access digitized materials, check the box marked "Descriptions of Archival Materials linked to digital copies." The website plans to expand but already provides an exceptional amount of government-sanctioned material.

### 7. Avalon Project at the Yale Law School: Documents in Law, History, and Government
*William C. Fray and Lisa A. Spar*
**http://www.yale.edu/lawweb/avalon/avalon.htm**

*Avalon* offers more than 3,500 full-text documents related to law, history, economics, politics, diplomacy, and government. Documents are divided into five time periods—pre-eighteenth century, eighteenth century, nineteenth century, twentieth century, and twenty-first century — and include treaties, presidential papers, and

Land advertisement from *American Time Capsule* [5].
*(Library of Congress)*

colonial charters, as well as state and federal constitutional and legal documents. Materials are also categorized into sixty-four document collections, such as *American Revolution, Federalist Papers, Slavery, Native Americans, Confederate States of America, World War II, Cold War, Indochina, Soviet-American Diplomacy,* and *September 11, 2001.* Material can also be accessed through an alphabetical list of 350 specific categories, keyword searching, and advanced searching. Although most of these documents are directly related to American history, the website includes a number of documents on ancient, medieval, Renaissance, European, and modern diplomatic history.

### 8. Built in America: Historic American Buildings Survey and Historic American Engineering Record
*Library of Congress, American Memory; National Parks Service*
http://memory.loc.gov/ammem/hhtml/hhhome.html

These facsimile images of measured drawings, photographs, and written documentation cover 10,000 significant historic sites dating from the seventeenth to the twentieth century. The *Historic American Buildings Survey (HABS)* started in 1933 as a work relief program and became a permanent part of the National Park Service the following year to document the architectural heritage of U.S. buildings. The *Historic American Engineering Record (HAER)* was established in 1969 to similarly survey engineering works and industrial websites. For each structure, the website provides up to ten drawings, thirty photographs, and fifty pages of *HABS* text detailing the structure's history, significance, and current condition.

### 9. Capital and the Bay: Narratives of Washington and the Chesapeake Bay Region, ca. 1600–1925

*Library of Congress, American Memory*
http://memory.loc.gov/ammem/lhcbhtml/lhcbhome.html

This website offers published books selected in an "attempt to capture in words and pictures a distinctive region as it developed" from European settlement to the early twentieth century. It contains 139 books, mostly by little-known residents and visitors to the region. A few were written by well-known figures, such as Edwin Booth, Frederick Douglass, and Thomas Jefferson. Materials include memoirs, autobiographies, biographies, letters, journals, poems, speeches, travel books, sermons, and promotional brochures. The cities of Baltimore and Richmond are also featured. The website includes ten works dealing with slavery — a number of which were written by former slaves — and approximately ten works dealing with encounters between whites and American Indians. There are links to twenty-two related websites.

### 10. Connecticut History Online

*Connecticut Historical Society, University of Connecticut, Mystic Seaport Museum, New Haven Colony Historical Society*
http://www.lib.uconn.edu/cho

This website offers approximately 14,000 images depicting Connecticut's history from the nineteenth to the middle of the twentieth century. The images are divided into five categories, each with two or three pertinent exhibits. *Livelihood* portrays the workplace, featuring the textile industry and maritime trades. *Diversity* depicts the state's racial, ethnic, and socioeconomic makeup, with an exhibit on women at work. *Lifestyle* captures everyday life, including rural and beach life. *Infrastructure* includes images of buildings, bridges, education, emergency services, and transportation, including features on natural disasters and war on the home front. *Environment* displays the state's natural and constructed landscapes and townscapes, including the many roles of the Connecticut River.

### 11. Democratic Vistas: The William Clyde DeVane Lecture Series

*Yale University*
http://www.yale.edu/yale300/democracy

In spring 2001, Yale University celebrated its tercentennial by assembling fifteen distinguished professors to lecture on "the conditions and prospects of democracy" in America. The complete lectures and discussions are available in text, audio, and video. Many lectures relate American democracy to a variety of historical subjects, including the market, family, religion, foreign policy, education, social movements, computers, and the biomedical revolution. Other topics include the widening income gap between rich and poor, the relation of Plato's *Republic* to the American Republic, Lincoln and Whitman as representative Americans, and whether citizenship is now dead. Reading lists are provided for each lecture.

### 12. Digital Archive of American Architecture
*Professor Jeffery Howe, Boston College*
http://www.bc.edu./bc_org/avp/cas/fnart/fa267

This website provides nearly 1,500 images of 280 architecturally significant American buildings from the colonial era to the present. Images of houses, churches, public buildings, commercial buildings, and skyscrapers are arranged according to period, location, architect, building type, and style. Images are included from three World's Fairs — the Centennial exposition in Philadelphia in 1876, Chicago's Columbian exposition in 1893, and the Louisiana Purchase exposition of 1904 in St. Louis — as well as sections on urban planning and comparative materials on European architecture. There are also digitized images and texts from two mid-nineteenth-century books on design and ornament. Annotations are minimal.

### 13. Digital History
*Steven Mintz and Sara McNeil, University of Houston*
http://www.digitalhistory.uh.edu/

These multimedia resources and links are designed to facilitate the study of U.S. history. This website presents more than 600 documents on the history of Mexican Americans, American Indians, and slavery, from "first encounters" through the Civil War. The website offers a complete U.S. history textbook, historical newspaper articles, and more than 1,500 annotated links, including 330 links to audio files of historic speeches and nine links to audio files of historians discussing relevant topics. There are ten essays on past controversies, such as the Vietnam War, socialism, and the war on poverty; seven essays presenting historical background on more recent controversies; and lengthy essays on the history of American film and private life in America. Exhibits offer 217 photographs from a freedmen's school in Alabama and seven letters written between eighteenth-century English historian Catharine Macaulay and American historian Mercy Otis Warren.

### 14. Digital Library of Georgia
*University of Georgia Libraries*
http://dlg.galileo.usg.edu

This website brings together a wealth of material from libraries, archives, and museums across Georgia. Legal materials include more than 17,000 state documents from 1794 to the present, updated daily, and a complete set of *Acts* and *Resolutions* from 1799 to 1995. *Southeastern Native American Documents* provides approximately 2,000 letters, legal documents, military orders, financial papers, and archaeological images from 1730 to 1842. Materials from the Civil War era include a soldier's diary and two collections of letters. The website provides a collection of eighty full-text versions of books from the early nineteenth century to the 1920s and three historic newspapers. There are approximately 2,500 political cartoons from 1946 to 1982; a firsthand account of civil unrest during an 1868 rally; Jimmy Carter's diaries of 1971

Civil War lithograph at *Digital History* [13].
*(Gilder-Lehrman Collection)*

to 1975 and 1977 to 1981; annual reports by the mayor of Savannah, 1865–1917; photographs of African Americans from Augusta during the late nineteenth century; and 1,500 architectural and landscape photographs from the 1940s to the 1980s.

### 15. Digital Scriptorium
*Rare Book, Manuscript, and Special Collections Library, Duke University*
http://scriptorium.lib.duke.edu

This website embraces twelve digitized collections, five exhibits, and six student projects, all containing primary documents. Collections include two websites related to advertising — *Emergence of Advertising in America, 1850–1920* [147] and *Ad\*Access* [180] — in addition to a collection of health-related ads from 1911 to 1958 in *Medicine and Madison Avenue* [160]. *George Percival Scriven: An American in Bohol, The Philippines, 1899–1901* presents a first-hand account by a U.S. officer of life during the occupation. *Civil War Women* offers correspondence and a diary relating to three American women of diverse backgrounds. *African American Women* presents letters by three slaves and a memoir by the daughter of slaves. *Emma Spaulding Bryant Letters* presents ten revealing letters written in 1873 by Mrs. Bryant to her husband concerning medical and private matters. *Historic American Sheet Music* includes more than 3,000 pieces published between 1850 and 1920. *Documents from the Women's Liberation Movement* offers more than forty documents from 1969 to 1974. *William Gedney Photographs and Writings* provides close to 5,000 prints, work prints, and contact sheets from the 1950s to the 1980s. *Urban Landscapes* presents more than 1,000 images depicting urban areas.

## 16. Election Statistics

*Office of the Clerk, U.S. House of Representatives*
http://clerk.house.gov/members/election_information/elections.php

Compiled from official sources, this website provides vote counts for nominees in all federal elections from 1920 to 2002. Statistics for elections prior to 1992 are available as scanned images of published documents in PDF format; results from elections held in 1992 and after are offered in HTML as well as PDF. Information on current House members and committees, as well as data on the makeup of the House in past Congresses, is easy to locate with links to each Congress's legislative activity. Special exhibits present a historical overview and fact sheet on the State of the Union address and information on addresses made by foreign dignitaries to joint sessions of Congress.

## 17. English Language Resources

*University of Virginia, Electronic Text Center*
http://etext.lib.virginia.edu/english.html

This website provides more than 9,500 full-text works. In addition to writings by Edgar Allan Poe and Walt Whitman, there are 322 works on or by African Americans; 133 works on or by American Indians; 467 titles by women writers; sixty-eight titles in *Early American Fiction*; and fifty-seven "best sellers" from 1900 to 1930. Nonliterary collections include the *Jackson Davis Collection of African American Education Photographs, 1910–1940*, with nearly 6,000 images of black schools throughout the South, and the *Philip S. Hench Walter Reed Yellow Fever Collection* of approximately 5,500 items on the conquest of the disease. The following University of Virginia *Electronic Text* websites are described in more detail in this book: *Diary, Correspondence, and Papers of Robert "King" Carter of Virginia, 1701–1732* [40], *Plymouth Colony Archive Project* [44], *Salem Witch Trials* [45], *Thomas Jefferson Digital Archive* [61], *Mark Twain in His Times* [124], and *Harlem: Mecca of the New Negro* [153].

## 18. Famous Trials

*Douglas Linder, Professor of Law, University of Missouri, Kansas City*
http://www.law.umkc.edu/faculty/projects/ftrials/ftrials.htm

This exceptional legal history website includes balanced treatment of thirty-five prominent court trials, including Salem witchcraft (1692); Boston Massacre (1770); Burr conspiracy (1807); *Amistad* (1839–1840); Dakota conflict (1862); Lincoln conspiracy (1865); Johnson impeachment (1868); Susan B. Anthony (1873); Bill Haywood (1907); Sacco and Vanzetti (1921); Scopes (1925); Scottsboro Boys (1931–1937); Rosenbergs (1951); Lenny Bruce (1964); "Mississippi Burning" (1967); Chicago Seven (1969–1970); My Lai courts martial (1970); LAPD officers (1992); and O. J. Simpson (1995). Each trial website includes historical background, biographies, and approximately fifteen to twenty-five primary documents, including transcripts of testimony, media coverage, depositions, and government documents. Most cases also contain images, links to related websites, and a bibliography. Biographies center on five "trial heroes," including Clarence Darrow. "Constitutional Conflicts" offers twenty-nine important constitutional topics for class discussion.

### 19. Historical Scholarship Online

| | |
|---|---|
| *JSTOR* | http://www.jstor.org |
| *Project Muse* | http://muse.jhu.edu |
| *History Cooperative* | http://www.historycooperative.org |
| *America: History and Life* | http://serials.abc-clio.com |

Three of these subscription services provide full-text access to important peer-reviewed academic history journals in addition to scholarly publications in related fields. The fourth, *America: History and Life*, furnishes bibliographic data for all major English-language historical journals. *JSTOR* offers page images from more than 350 scholarly journals (about forty of them in history), some going back to the nineteenth century. Issues from the past three to five years are not generally available. *Project MUSE* offers current issues and coverage from the recent past — going back as far as 1993 — in PDF and HTML formats from more than 220 journals,

Paul Revere's engraving of the Boston Massacre at *Famous Trials* [18].
*(Anne S. K. Brown Military Collection)*

including forty-one categorized under "History." Linked searches are provided for twenty-five titles found in *JSTOR* and *Project MUSE*. The *History Cooperative* presents recent issues from 1999 to the most current for a dozen major history journals — including the *American Historical Review* and the *Journal of American History. America: History and Life* contains more than 450,000 entries with abstracts and indexing for all articles and reviews from more than 2,000 journals from 1964 to the present. All four websites offer keyword and Boolean searching.

## 20. History Books Online

*History E-Book Project, American Council of Learned Societies*
http://www.historyebook.org

*Net Library, OCLC Online Computer Library Center, Inc.*
http://www.netlibrary.com

*Questia, Questia Media America, Inc.*
http://www.questia.com

These subscription services offer full-text scholarly books selected for their importance in academic humanities disciplines. The *History E-Book Project* furnishes 750 titles, more than 280 related to U.S. history. More than half of the books were published within the past three decades, so the selection of titles is representative of recent scholarship. The project plans to add 250 titles annually over the next few years, as well as eighty-five electronic books created to take advantage of Internet technology for scholarly purposes. *Net Library* offers more than 63,000 full-text scholarly, professional, and reference ebooks from more than 359 publishers. Individuals may view material online or "check out" items — with exclusive use — for twenty-four hours. Users can download one page at a time and search through all volumes for words, names, and subjects. *Questia*, geared for student research, allows subscribing institutions access to more than 47,000 books and 375,000 journals, magazines, and newspaper articles from more than 235 publishers. It also offers individual subscriptions. Unlike users of *Net Library*, *Questia* users do not "check out" books or download material. *Questia* provides highlighting and margin note functions in addition to a "personalized workspace" with automatic footnoting and compiling of bibliographies.

## 21. History Matters: The U.S. Survey Course on the Web

*Center for History and New Media, George Mason University; and American Social History Project/CML, City University of New York*
http://historymatters.gmu.edu/

This website provides a host of resources for teachers and students in U.S. History survey courses. Three features are particularly useful for students: *WWW.History*, *Many Pasts*, and *Making Sense of Evidence. WWW.History* provides an annotated guide to more than 700 high-quality websites covering all of U.S. history. Users can browse websites by time period or topic and can search by keyword. *Many Pasts* offers more than 1,000 primary sources in text, image, and audio, from an exchange between Powhatan and Captain John Smith to a 1928 song about domestic service called "Sadie's Servant Room Blues" to comments by the director of the Arab-

American Family Support Center in Brooklyn after the September 11, 2001, terrorist attacks. *Making Sense of Evidence* offers eight guides with interactive exercises designed to help students learn to analyze various kinds of primary sources, including maps, early film, oral history, and popular songs. These guides offer questions to ask and provide examples of how to analyze kinds of evidence. There are also eight multimedia modules, based on interviews with prominent scholars, that model strategies for analyzing primary sources, including political cartoons, blues, and abolitionist speeches. Additional features include *Past Meets Present*, a series of essays placing current events in historical perspective, and *Reference Desk*, an annotated guide to websites on citing digital resources, copyright and fair use information, evaluating digital resources, and standards. *Students as Historians* highlights examples of quality student work on the Internet.

### 22. History News Network (HNN)

*Rick Shenkman, Editor*

http://hnn.us

This weekly, web-based magazine features articles by historians of all political persuasions and places current events in historical perspective. Historians and people interested in the intersection of the past and the present compose the central audience. Special features include *Breaking News* (related to history); *Roundup,* a weekly compendium of media excerpts concerning history and news; *blogs* (web logs) written by historians; and *Grapevine,* a monthly summary of news involving historians. HNN's archive, currently with more than 1,600 entries, is searchable by keyword, author, HNN department, or date. The website is valuable for linking the study of the past with present-day public concerns.

### 23. History Teacher's Bag of Tricks: Adventures in Roland Marchand's File Cabinet

*Area 3 History and Cultures Project*

http://marchand.ucdavis.edu

A memorial to Roland Marchand, historian of popular culture and advertising, this website presents a slide library with more than 6,100 images, including more than 2,000 advertisements, drawn from Marchand's collection. Images are organized into forty-one major categories and 191 subcategories. The website also offers forty-eight lesson plans designed by Marchand, each with an introduction, essay assignment, and primary source documents. The website will be useful for researching popular culture and advertising, along with many other topics in American history, from the Puritans through Watergate.

### 24. Hypertext on American History from the Colonial Period until Modern Times

*Professor George M. Welling, University Groningen (Netherlands),
University Bergen (Norway)*

http://odur.let.rug.nl/~usa/usa.htm

This website provides more than 375 documents related to U.S. history from the colonial period to the present. *Essays* contains more than thirty-five writings on various aspects of U.S. history. *Biographies* offers more than 200 biographies of historical figures related to American history, ranging from 350 words to 2,000 words in length. *Presidents* contains documents pertaining to each U.S. president. Documents and essays are hyperlinked to four editions of the booklet *An Outline of American History* (1954, 1963, 1990, and 1994), a publication distributed abroad by the United States Information Service, along with similar volumes on American economy, government, literature, and geography.

## 25. Indian Affairs: Laws and Treaties
*Oklahoma University Library, Digital Publications*
http://digital.library.okstate.edu/kappler

This digitized version of *Indian Affairs: Laws and Treaties* is a valuable resource. *Indian Affairs* is a highly regarded, seven-volume compendium of treaties, laws, and executive orders relating to United States–Indian affairs. It was originally compiled by Charles J. Kappler in 1904 and was updated through 1970. *Volume Two* presents treaties signed between 1778 and 1882. *Volumes I* and *III–VII* cover laws, executive and departmental orders, and important court decisions involving American Indians from 1871 to 1970. Some volumes also provide tribal fund information. This version includes the editor's margin notations, as well as detailed index entries, and allows searches across volumes. This is a comprehensive resource for legal documents on U.S. relations with American Indians.

## 26. Kentuckiana Digital Library
*Kentucky Virtual Library*
http://www.kyvl.org/kentuckiana/digilibcoll/digilibcoll.shtml

A collection of historical material from fifteen Kentucky colleges, universities, libraries, and historical societies. It includes nearly 8,000 photographs; ninety-five full-text books, manuscripts, and journals from 1784 to 1971; ninety-four oral histories; seventy-eight issues of *Mountain Life and Work* from 1925 to 1962; and twenty-two issues of *Works Progress Administration in Kentucky: Narrative Reports*. Photographs include collections by Russell Lee, who documented health conditions resulting from coal industry practices; Roy Stryker, head of the New Deal Farm Security Administration photographic section; and others that provide images of cities, towns, schools, camps, and disappearing cultures. Oral histories address Supreme Court Justice Stanley F. Reed, Senator John Sherman Cooper, the Frontier Nursing Service, veterans, fiddlers, and the transition from farming to an industrial economy. Texts include Civil War diaries, religious tracts, speeches, correspondence, and scrapbooks. Documents cover a range of topics, including colonization societies, civil rights, education, railroads, feuding, the Kentucky Derby, Daniel Boone, and a personal recollection of Abraham Lincoln.

## 27. LexisNexis
*Reed Elsevier, Inc.*
http://www.lexisnexis.com

This subscription service provides full-text and keyword searching to more than 5,900 news, business, legal, medical, and reference publications. The database

Early nitrate photograph of University of Kentucky Dean F. Paul Anderson with his dogs at *Kentuckiana Digital Library* [26].
*(Nollau Nitrate Photographic Print Collection, University of Kentucky Libraries)*

accesses current and recent issues of more than fifty major English-language newspapers, including the *New York Times* and the *Washington Post* back to 1980 or earlier. The database also offers more than 400 magazines and journals, 600 newsletters, and transcripts of radio and television broadcasts from major networks. Legal materials include federal and state cases, laws, codes, regulations, and law review articles. Business resources include SEC filings and reports and corporate financial information and profiles. The site also provides statistical tables of data pertaining to industries, biographical information, country and state profiles, polls and surveys, and the *World Almanac* and *Book of Facts*. Access to various parts of this enormous resource varies by subscription agreement.

## 28. Library of Virginia Digital Library Program

*Library of Virginia*
http://www.lva.lib.va.us/dlp

This website offers access to tens of thousands of digitized documents and photographs as well as sixteen exhibits on Virginia history. Users can find more than 26,000 photographs that document buildings and people, including 1,500 photos related to African American life in the *Lee F. Rodgers Collection*. Additional resources include patents and grants submitted to the Virginia Land Office between 1623 and 1992. Northern Neck Grants and Survey forms filed between 1692 and 1892 are available, as are military records, including Revolutionary War state pensions and World War I History Commission Questionnaires. The website offers WPA Life histories (1,350 oral histories) and Virginia religious petitions from 1774 to 1802. Exhibits deal with the legacy of the New Deal in Virginia, resistance to slavery, Virginia roots music (with seven audio selections), Thomas Jefferson, John Marshall, coal towns, and political life.

### 29. Map Collections: 1500–2003
*Library of Congress, American Memory*
http://memory.loc.gov/ammem/gmdhtml/gmdhome.html

This large collection of maps from the sixteenth century to the present focuses on Americana and "cartographic treasures." Materials are organized into seven thematic categories — *Cities and Towns*; *Conservation and Environment*; *Discovery and Exploration*; *Cultural Landscapes*; *Military Battles and Campaigns*; *Transportation and Communication*; and *General Maps*. Sections include a number of special presentations with essays on *George Washington: Surveyor and Mapmaker*, the *1562 Map of America by Diego Gutiérrez*, and *National Atlases: Presenting the Nation's Cultural Geography*. Users may zoom in to view details and download maps. Specific map collections of particular importance for studying American history include *Discovery and Exploration*; *The American Revolution and Its Era*; *Railroad Maps, 1828–1900*; *American Colonization Society Collection: Maps of Liberia, 1830–1870*; *Panoramic Maps, 1847–1929*; *Civil War Maps*; and *Mapping the National Parks*.

### 30. MATRIX: The Center for Humane Arts, Letters, and Social Sciences Online
*H-Net, Michigan State University*
http://www.h-net.org/

H-Net, an international interdisciplinary organization, provides this indispensable historical resource focused primarily on the needs of teachers and scholars. *H-Net Reviews* publishes and disseminates reviews of books, films, museums, software, sound recordings, and websites. *Discussion Networks* is a gateway to more than 130 academic discussion networks administered by H-Net via email. *H-Net Papers on Teaching and Technology* presents ten discussion panels on multimedia teaching. The website also provides academic announcements of professional organizations, conference programs, fellowships, and prizes as well as employment listings and additional websites from various H-Net special projects.

### 31. Ohio Memory: An Online Scrapbook of Ohio History
*Ohio Memory Project*
http://www.ohiomemory.org

This wealth of material from archives, libraries, and museums currently includes more than 24,000 images that document Ohio life, culture, and history from prehistoric times to the recent past. The website provides 2,166 audiovisual items, 742 historical objects, artifacts, or buildings, eighty-one natural history specimens, 669 published works, and 628 collections of unpublished material. Users can browse or search by word, place, and subject. Results are presented chronologically on scrapbook pages with ten selections per page. *Learning Resources* offers twenty-two categories of illustrated essays. Topics include African Americans, agriculture, American Indians, arts and entertainment, business and labor, civil liberties, daily life, education, immigration and ethnic heritage, government, religion, science and technology, sports, and women.

## 32. Online Archive of California
*University of California*
http://www.oac.cdlib.org/texts

This impressive archive provides more than 81,000 images and 1,000 texts on the history and culture of California. Images may be searched by keyword or browsed according to six categories: history, nature, people, places, society, and technology. Topics include exploration, Indians, gold rushes, and California events. Three collections of texts are also available. *Japanese American Relocation Digital Archive* furnishes 309 documents and sixty-seven oral histories. *Free Speech Movement: Student Protest, U.C. Berkeley, 1964–1965* provides 541 documents, including books, letters, press releases, oral histories, photographs, and trial transcripts. *UC Berkeley Regional Oral History Office* offers full-text transcripts of 139 interviews organized into fourteen topics including agriculture, arts, California government, society and family life, wine industry, disability rights, Earl Warren, Jewish community leaders, medicine (including AIDS), suffragists, and U.C. black alumni.

## 33. ProQuest Information and Learning
*ProQuest Company*
http://www.umi.com/proquest/

This subscription service provides a variety of valuable resources for history students. First, it offers a large number of secondary sources, including more than 2,500 scholarly journals, magazines, newspapers, and trade publications, with full-text access and searching capabilities for approximately half of these. Second, *ProQuest Historical Newspapers* series offers an enormous body of primary sources, including access to the following: the *New York Times* (1851–2001), the *Washington Post* (1877–1988), the *Wall Street Journal* (1889–1986), the *Christian Science Monitor* (1908–1991), and the *Los Angeles Times* (1881–1984). For researching topics in recent history, *ProQuest* provides recent issues — going back to the 1980s in some cases — from more than 500 newspapers worldwide. These include specialized publications from the worlds of business, education, medicine, religion, and sciences and reference resources. Keyword and Boolean searching, with limitations by publication and date, are available in addition to browse topics organized by subject, persons, locations, and company names. Because *ProQuest* offers subscribers a variety of product "modules," the materials just described may not be available at all institutions.

## 34. SCETI: Schoenberg Center for Electronic Text and Image
*University of Pennsylvania Special Collections Library*
http://dewey.library.upenn.edu/sceti

This eclectic collection of more than 2,200 items spans the seventeenth to the twentieth centuries. Visitors can search material from nine sections and visit fourteen exhibitions. *A Crisis of the Union* presents 224 pamphlets, broadsides, clippings, paintings, and maps to address the "causes, conduct, and consequences" of the Civil War. A collection devoted to Theodore Dreiser presents correspondence, various editions of the novel *Sister Carrie*, an early manuscript for *Jennie Gerhardt*, and scholarly essays. An exhibit with more than forty audio and video recordings complements a collection of approximately 4,000 photographs from singer Marian Anderson's papers. A collection on the history of chemistry emphasizes the pre-1850 period with monographs and more than 3,000 images of scientists, laboratories, and apparatus; another exhibit emphasizes the ENIAC computer. See also *Cultural Readings: Colonization and Print in the Americas* [39].

## 35. United States Historical Census Data Browser
*Geospatial and Statistical Data Center, University of Virginia Library*
http://fisher.lib.virginia.edu/collections/stats/histcensus

This website provides extensive data from census records and other government sources. For each decade between 1790 and 1960, users can browse population and economic statistical information at state and county levels. Data can be arranged according to a variety of categories, including place of birth, age, gender, marital status, race, ethnicity, education, illiteracy, salary levels, and housing. Variables also include specifics dealing with agriculture, labor, and manufacturing such as material costs and crop values. Users can select up to fifteen variables when conducting searches, and the website displays results as both raw data and statistical charts. Categories are inconsistent between census periods and even within particular periods, providing a rich resource for studying how census questions have changed over time. The website includes a lengthy essay on the history of American censuses. This database is a great statistical resource for students of American history. Additional but less user-friendly data focused on social history are available at *Integrated Public Use Microdata Series* (http://www.ipums.umn.edu).

## 36. Women and Social Movements in the United States, 1775–2000
*Thomas Dublin and Kathryn Kish Sklar*
http://womhist.binghamton.edu.

This website offers forty-five "mini-monographs," each consisting of a background essay and relevant primary source documents, organized around analytical questions concerning social movements. Projects are organized into five subject categories: peace and international; politics and public life; sexuality, reproduction, and women's health; work and production; and race and gender. The website includes more than 1,000 documents and 400 photographs. Keyword searching, links to more than 400 websites, and more than twenty-four lesson plans are also provided. The website is expanding to include thousands of new documents starting in the year 1600 in a joint project with *Alexander Street Press* [2]. The joint website will charge a subscription fee for access to new documents and to half of the current projects, but the other half will remain free.

# U.S. HISTORY WEBSITES BY TIME PERIOD

## Three Worlds Meet and Colonization, Beginnings to 1763

### 37. Atlantic Slave Trade and Slave Life in the Americas: A Visual Record
*Jerome Handler and Michael Tuite Jr., University of Virginia*
http://hitchcock.itc.virginia.edu/Slavery

More than 900 images depict the enslavement of Africans, the Atlantic slave trade, and slave life in the New World. Images are arranged into eighteen categories, including precolonial Africa, capture of slaves, maps, slave ships, plantation scenes, physical punishment, music, free people of color, family life, religion, marketing, rebellion, and emancipation. Many of the images are from seventeenth- and eighteenth-century books and travel accounts, but some are taken from sketches within slave narratives, *Harper's Weekly*, and *Monthly Magazine*. Reference information and brief comments, often an excerpt from the original captions, accompany each image. Although there is no interpretation or discussion of historical relevance, these images are valuable for learning about representations of slavery in American slave societies, especially in the Caribbean and Latin America.

### 38. Colonial Connecticut Records, 1636–1776
*University of Connecticut Libraries*
http://www.colonialct.uconn.edu

This website offers a scanned and partially searchable version of the fifteen-volume *Public Records of the Colony of Connecticut from April 1636 to October 1776*, originally published between 1850 and 1890. Users can search documents by date, volume, and page number. Each of the fifteen volumes, which cover successive time periods, includes alphabetical, hyperlinked subject terms for browsing. The website also provides access by type of material: charters, documents, inventories, laws, letters, and court proceedings. Keyword searching may be available in the future, but even without this option, the website offers a wealth of accessible material on politics, legal matters, Indian affairs, military actions, social concerns, agriculture, religion, and other aspects of early Connecticut history.

### 39. Cultural Readings: Colonization and Print in the Americas
*University of Pennsylvania Library*
http://www.library.upenn.edu/special/gallery/kislak/index/cultural.html

Texts about the Americas produced in Europe from the fifteenth through the nineteenth centuries are examined in this exhibit. Approximately 100 images of printed texts, drawings, artworks, and maps from published and unpublished sources are arranged into six thematic categories: *Promotion and Possession; Viewers and the*

*Viewed*; *Print and Native Cultures*; *Religion and Print*; *New World Lands in Print*; and *Colonial Fictions, Colonial Histories*. Three scholarly essays contextualize the documents. A bibliography with thirty-six titles and twenty-five links accompany the presentation. This is a visually attractive, thoughtful website that explores connections between colonization and representation.

### 40. Diary, Correspondence, and Papers of Robert "King" Carter of Virginia, 1701–1732
*Edmund Berkeley Jr., University of Virginia*
http://etext.lib.virginia.edu/users/berkeley

A work-in-progress, this collection offers letters and diary entries by Robert "King" Carter (1663–1732), a wealthy landowner and leading public figure in Virginia. Educated in England, Carter inherited and acquired more than 300,000 acres in the Northern Neck Proprietary between the Rappahannock and Potomac rivers. Carter, who owned nearly 1,000 slaves, served as a member of the Council of Virginia and as acting governor of the colony. The website presently contains approximately 400 letters, written between 1701 and 1727, diary entries covering 1722 to 1726, and wills. Each document provides both modern and original spellings as well as hyperlinked notes with identifying information for more than 130 persons, places, and things. The website also offers a 2,200-word biography of Carter, a 2,100-word essay on the Northern Neck Proprietary, and a bibliography of seventy titles. These materials are useful for studying eighteenth-century aristocratic, political, and economic life in Virginia.

### 41. Geography of Slavery in America
*Virginia Center for Digital History and University of Virginia, Wise*
http://www.vcdh.virginia.edu/gos

This website provides transcriptions and images of more than 2,400 newspaper advertisements between 1736 and 1777 regarding runaway slaves. The runaways are primarily from Virginia but also come from states along the eastern seaboard and locations abroad. Materials include ads placed by owners and overseers as well as those for captured or suspected runaway slaves placed by sheriffs and other governmental officials. Additional advertisements announce runaway servants, sailors, and military deserters. The website provides approximately forty documents on runaways, including letters, laws, court documents, planters' records, and literature. Ten photographs of a re-created slave dwelling, information on currency and clothing of the time, a gazetteer with seven maps of the region, and a bibliography with thirteen titles are also available. This is a valuable source for studying slave culture, Virginia in the eighteenth century, and the use of print culture to support the institution of slavery.

Runaway advertisement from *Georgraphy of Slavery in America* [41].
(The Geography of Slavery, *Virginia Center for Digital History*)

## 42. New Perspectives on the West

*Public Broadcasting Service*

http://www3.pbs.org/weta/thewest

This educational resource complements the eight-part PBS documentary series *The West* by Ken Burns and Stephen Ives. The website is organized into several sections: a guided tour of the West; an interactive timeline to 1917; a hypertext map that includes migration and commerce routes, games and puzzles; and, most importantly, archival materials collected during the making of the series. Primary sources — fifty-six documents and 148 images — are organized in chronological order and include memoirs, letters, government reports, and photographs. Despite the website's title, it does not offer new perspectives on the American West offered recently by historians or in-depth discussion of issues such as gender or the environment. Political and military history and, to a lesser extent, social and ethnic history, however, are well represented in this account, which begins with sixteenth-century European expeditions and ends at the start of the twentieth century.

## 43. Old Mobile Archaeology

*Center for Archaeological Studies, University of South Alabama*

http://www.usouthal.edu/archaeology/old_mobile.htm

This well-designed website showcases the work of archaeologists in their excavations at Mobile and elsewhere in Alabama. Visitors can "virtually visit" archaeological websites in the town of Old Mobile, capital of the French colony of Louisiane from 1702 to 1711; the Mississippian Indian city of Bottle Creek (1100–1400); the Indian fishing website of Dauphin Island Shell Mounds (1100–1550); the French village of Port Dauphin (1702–1725); the Dog River Plantation website, home to a French Canadian immigrant family, numerous Indians, and slaves (1720s–1848); and websites in downtown Mobile, including a Spanish colonial house (ca. 1800), an early-nineteenth-century riverfront tavern, and antebellum cotton warehouses. *Artifacts* features more than 250 images of pottery shards with accompanying descriptions. The website includes images and information on seven additional French colonial websites in Nova Scotia, New York, Michigan, Illinois, Mississippi, and Louisiana. These materials demonstrate the value of archaeology for historical research.

## 44. Plymouth Colony Archive Project

*Patricia Scott Deetz, Christopher Fennell, and J. Eric Deetz, University of Virginia*

http://etext.lib.virginia.edu/users/deetz

A wealth of documents and analytical essays emphasize the social history of Plymouth Colony from 1620 to 1691. This website also offers a tribute to the scholarly work of the late James Deetz, professor of historical archaeology. Documents include 135 probates, twenty-four wills, and twelve texts containing laws and court cases on land division, master-servant relations, sexual misconduct, and disputes involving American Indians. The website also provides approximately eighty biographical studies, research papers, and topical articles that analyze "life ways" of 395 individuals who lived in the colony and offer theoretical views on the colony's legal structure, women's roles, vernacular house forms, and domestic violence. There are nineteen maps or plans, approximately fifty photographs, and excerpts from Deetz's books on the history and myths of Plymouth Colony and on Anglo-American gravestone styles. These materials are valuable for learning about historical anthropology, material culture, and American colonial history.

### 45. Salem Witch Trials: Documentary Archive and Transcription Project
*Benjamin Ray, University of Virginia*
**http://etext.virginia.edu/salem/witchcraft**

This comprehensive website focuses on the Salem witch trials of 1692. It provides full-text versions of the three-volume, verbatim Salem witch trial transcripts, an extensive seventeenth-century narrative of the trials, and full-text pamphlets and excerpts of sermons by Cotton Mather, Robert Calef, and Thomas Maule. It also offers four full-text rare books written in the late seventeenth and early eighteenth centuries about the witchcraft scare. Access is provided to more than 500 documents from the collections of the Essex County Court Archives and the Essex Institute Collection, and to roughly 100 primary documents housed in other archives. There are five maps of Salem and nearby villages. Basic information on the history of Salem/Danvers is complemented by seven related images and a fifty-word description of fourteen historical websites in Danvers. This website is a rich resource for researching the Salem witch hysteria.

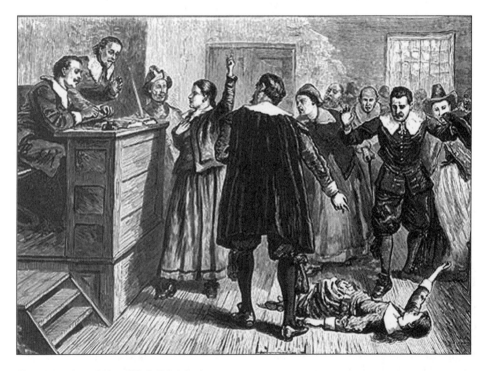

Illustration from *Salem Witch Trials* [45].
*(University of Virginia Library)*

Early map from *Virtual Jamestown* [46].
*(Virginia Center for Digital History)*

## 46. Virtual Jamestown

*Crandall Shifflett, Virginia Center for Digital History*
http://jefferson.village.virginia.edu/vcdh/jamestown

A work-in-progress, *Virtual Jamestown* is a good place to begin exploring the history of Jamestown. Due to be completed by 2007, the 400th anniversary of Jamestown's founding, the website at present includes sixty-three letters and firsthand accounts from 1570 to 1720 on voyages, settlements, Bacon's Rebellion, and early history as well as 100 public records, such as census data and laws. Additional materials include thirty maps and images, a registry of servants sent to plantations from 1654 to 1686, records from 1607 to 1815 of Christ's Hospital in England (where orphans were trained to apprentice in the colonies), and two indenture contracts. The website provides four interactive, virtual re-creations. The reference section includes a timeline from 1502 to the present, narratives by prominent historians, links to fifteen related websites, a bibliography of twenty primary and secondary sources, and a searchable database on Atlantic world studies resources.

# Revolution and the New Nation, 1754–1820s

## 47. Center on Religion and Democracy

*James Davison Hunter, University of Virginia Library*
http://religionanddemocracy.lib.virginia.edu

Designed to promote the study of religion and public life, this website offers classical, historical, religious, and legal works as well as *The Hedgehog Review*, an interdisciplinary journal. All texts are searchable by keyword. *Social Theory* contains twenty-nine texts, including writings by Ralph Waldo Emerson, Thomas Hobbes, John Locke, Karl Marx, and Plato. *Historical Texts* contains writings by eleven authors, including nine works by Frederick Douglass, five by W. E. B. Du Bois, five by Harriet Beecher Stowe, twelve by Booker T. Washington, and the complete *Writings of George Washington from the Original Manuscript Sources. Religious Texts* include the Koran, *The Book of Mormon*, two versions of the Bible, and texts by John Calvin and Martin Luther. *Legal Documents* contains twenty-three works, including the *Constitution of the Iroquois Nation* and writings by James Madison and George Mason.

## 48. Century of Lawmaking for a New Nation: Congressional Documents and Debates, 1774–1873
*Library of Congress, American Memory*
http://memory.loc.gov/ammem/amlaw/lawhome.html

A comprehensive set of congressional documents from the nation's founding through early Reconstruction is available on this website. Materials are organized into four categories: *Continental Congress and the Constitutional Convention; Statutes and Documents; Journals of Congress;* and *Debates of Congress.* The website provides descriptions of sixteen types of documents, including bills and resolutions, *American State Papers*, the *U.S. Serial Set, Journals of the Continental Congress*, the *Congressional Globe*, and the *Congressional Record.* A presentation on the making of the Constitution introduces an 1834 compilation of Congressional debates and proceedings, and a timeline presents American history as seen in congressional documents. Special attention is directed to Revolutionary-era diplomatic correspondence, Indian land cessions, the Louisiana Purchase, the *Journal of the Congress of the Confederate States of America, 1861–1865*, the impeachment of Andrew Johnson, and the electoral college.

## 49. Continental Congress and the Constitutional Convention
*Library of Congress, American Memory*
http://memory.loc.gov/ammem/bdsds/bdsdhome.html

Drafts and final versions of foundational U.S. government documents can be found on this website consisting of 253 broadsides relating to the Continental Congress (1774–1789) and twenty-one to the Constitutional Convention of 1787. Materials in the former group — most of which date from 1781 to 1788 — function as supplements to the better-known *Journals of the Continental Congress* by showing the development of legislation. Documents in the latter group relate to the ratification of a new Constitution to replace the Articles of Confederation. Most broadsides are one sheet, although some are as lengthy as twenty-eight pages. A special presentation, "To Form a More Perfect Union," presents selected documents within the historical context of organizing a war, encouraging patriotism, incorporating western territories following Britain's defeat, relations with Indians, identifying problems with the Confederation, and drafting the Constitution.

## 50. Doing History: Martha Ballard's Diary Online
*Film Study Center, Harvard University*
http://DoHistory.org

This rich site explores the eighteenth-century diary of midwife Martha Ballard and the construction of two late-twentieth-century historical studies based on the diary: historian Laurel Thatcher Ulrich's book *A Midwife's Tale* and Laurie Kahn-Leavitt's PBS film of the same name. The website provides facsimile and transcribed full-text versions of the 1,400-page diary. An archive offers images of more than 300 documents on such topics as Ballard's life, midwifery, birth, medical information, religion, and Maine history. Also included are three maps, present-day images of Augusta and Hallowell, Maine, and a timeline tracing Maine's history. The website offers suggestions on using primary sources to conduct research with ten essays on organizing projects and developing skills such as reading eighteenth-century writing, reading probate records, searching for deeds, and exploring graveyards. There are two in-depth case studies of how to do history.

### 51. Drafting the Documents of Independence
*Library of Congress*
http://lcweb.loc.gov/exhibits/declara/declara1.html

Eight documents and prints relating to the creation of the Declaration of Independence are presented, including a June 1826 letter from Thomas Jefferson to Roger C. Weightman that is "considered one of the sublime exaltations of individual and national liberty." Documents also include a fragment of the "earliest known draft of the Declaration of Independence," Thomas Jefferson's "original Rough draught" of the Declaration with later changes made by John Adams, Benjamin Franklin, and

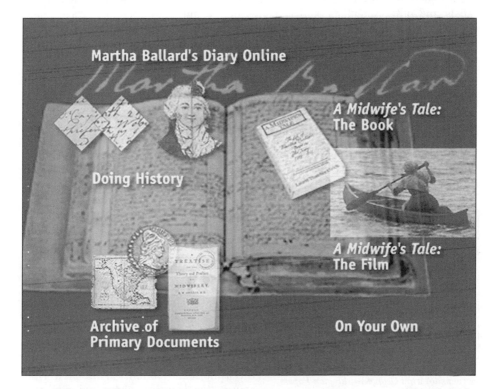

Screenshot from *Doing History: Martha Ballard's Diary Online* [50].
*(Doing History)*

others, and a portion of George Washington's copy of the "Dunlap Broadside" of the Declaration, read to his troops in New York on July 9, 1776. A print shows Washington's troops reacting to the reading by destroying a statue of King George III. A background essay and a chronology of events from June 7, 1776, to January 18, 1777, are also available. This website is well organized to present evidence of the Declaration's development and effect.

### 52. First American West: The Ohio River Valley, 1750–1820

*Library of Congress, American Memory; University of Chicago Library;*
*Filson Historical Society*

http://memory.loc.gov/ammem/award99/icuhtml/fawhome.html

This website provides approximately 15,000 pages of materials related to European migration into the Ohio River Valley during the latter half of the eighteenth century and beginning of the nineteenth. Materials include books, pamphlets, newspapers, periodicals, journals, letters, legal documents, pictorial images, maps, and ledgers. The website includes a special presentation with a 6,500-word hyperlink-filled essay on contested lands, peoples and migration, empires and politics, western life and culture, and the construction of a western past. Materials address encounters between Europeans and native peoples, the lives of African American slaves, the role of institutions such as churches and schools, the position of women, the thoughts of naturalists and other scientists, and activities of the migrants, including travel, land acquisition, planting, navigation of rivers, and trade. These are valuable resources for studying early American history, cross-cultural encounters, frontier history, and the construction of the nation's past.

### 53. George Washington Papers, 1741–1799

*Library of Congress, American Memory*

http://memory.loc.gov/ammem/gwhtml

This collection of approximately 65,000 documents written by or to George Washington is the largest set of original Washington documents in the world. It includes correspondence, letter books, diaries, journals, account books, military records, reports, and notes from 1741 through 1799. Although the website is searchable by keyword, many documents are available only as page images rather than as transcribed text, and the handwriting can be difficult to read. Transcripts do exist for all diary pages and for selected documents. The website includes a timeline with annotations to relevant documents; essays on Washington's diaries, letter books, and career as a surveyor and mapmaker; and an essay entitled "Creating the American Nation." This is a rich source for learning about colonial and early republic history.

Screenshot from *George Washington Papers, 1741–1799* [53].
*(Library of Congress)*

## 54. Interpreting the Declaration of Independence by Translation
*Center for History and New Media, George Mason University*
http://chnm.gmu.edu/declaration

The complex practice of translating historical documents is explored in this website, which provides eleven translations of the American Declaration of Independence into Behasa Melayu (Malay language), French, German, Hebrew, Italian, Japanese, Polish, Russian, and Spanish, along with sixteen essays that discuss these and other translations. The website reproduces a *Journal of American History* roundtable, published in March 1999, and includes introductory essays that discuss the endeavor of placing American history into a transnational perspective. Five "retranslations" back to English are of particular interest. This website is valuable for investigating the Declaration and historical interpretation.

## 55. Jefferson's Blood
*PBS Online and WGBH/Frontline*
http://www.pbs.org/wgbh/pages/frontline/shows/jefferson

This website extends a PBS *Frontline* program exploring the claim that Thomas Jefferson fathered at least one, and perhaps all, of the children of his slave, Sally Hemmings. This view is supported by DNA testing and believed to be valid by a consensus of historians and experts. The website presents ten in-depth essays by prominent historians and other scholars on the controversy, its historical background and significance, interracial sex in the antebellum Chesapeake region, Jefferson's legacy, and America's mixed-race heritage. The website provides accounts by four Monticello slaves and the chief overseer and four video segments, from seven to nine minutes each. Additional materials include transcripts of interviews with scholars who designed and carried out the testing and with Lucia Cinder Stanton from the Thomas Jefferson Memorial Foundation as well as links to information that argues against the claim.

## 56. Oneida Indian Nation: Culture and History
*Oneida Indian Nation*
http://oneida-nation.net/historical.html

The Oneida Indian Nation was called the "first ally and steadfast friend" of the fledgling American Republic. This website presents documents and studies focusing on the Revolutionary War period and the Oneida Nation's recent efforts to pursue land claims. Materials include six treaties or agreements involving the Oneida and the United States between 1777 and 1794, statements by presidents, Congress, and New York State, and Bill Clinton's 1994 memo on relations with tribal governments. The website also offers six essays by Oneida Nation historians and others on topics such as roles the Oneida played in the birth of the United States and in the War of 1812 and the land claim issue. Additional materials include excerpts from an oral history project in which thirteen tribal elders discuss food, herbal cures, crafts, language, and land claims, as well as essays on lacrosse, legends, and the tribal creation story. These resources are useful for studying American Indian history, the Revolutionary War period, and land claims efforts.

## 57. Osher Map Library
*Smith Center for Cartographic Education, University of Southern Maine*
http://www.usm.maine.edu/maps/web_exhibit.html

These fourteen exhibitions include more than 600 maps and related documents on aspects of history revealed through the study of maps. The website provides well-integrated essays of up to 8,000 words for each exhibit and some annotated bibliographies. Exhibits focusing on American history include *Mapping the Republic,* on conflicting conceptualizations of the United States from 1790 to 1900; *Exodus and Exiles,* on Diaspora experiences of Jews and African Americans; *The American Way,* a collection of twentieth-century road maps and guidebooks; *Carto-Maine-ia,* on popular uses of maps; and *Maine Wilderness Transformed,* which examines "the creation of a landscape of exploitation." In addition, *The Cartographic Creation of New England,* addresses European exploration and settlement; *The "Percy Map"* presents a significant Revolutionary War map; and *John Mitchell's Map* offers insight into diplomatic disputes. These maps are especially valuable for studying exploration and cartography in American history.

## 58. Papers of John Jay
*Columbia University*
http://www.columbia.edu/cu/lweb/eresources/archives/jay

A compilation of the unpublished papers of founder John Jay, dating from 1745 to 1829, this website comprises nearly 14,000 pages scanned from Jay's manuscripts and related materials. The primary documents have not yet been transcribed and are difficult to read in the original, although users can enlarge and enhance the documents. The correspondence from such prominent individuals as John Adams, Benjamin Franklin, Alexander Hamilton, Thomas Jefferson, and George Washington deals with New York, antislavery, repeal of the Missouri Compromise, international affairs, state government, and politics. Records are searchable by keyword, name of writer, and date. Materials include abstracts, bibliographic notes, and thematic essays with hyperlinks to documents on Jay and New York, France, slavery, and the 1794 treaty with Britain that bears his name. The website also includes a 1,300-word biography and a bibliography of more than fifty relevant sources.

## 59. Religion and the Founding of the American Republic
*Library of Congress*
http://lcweb.loc.gov/exhibits/religion/religion.html

This exhibition of 212 written documents and visual images explores the significance of religion for early American history. Materials include manuscripts, letters, books, prints, paintings, artifacts, and music. Seven sections — each including a 500-word essay and brief annotations for each object displayed — cover the following topics: religious persecution in Europe that led to emigration; religious experience in eighteenth-century America, including the Great Awakening; the influence of religious leaders and ideas on the War of Independence; policies toward religion of the Continental Confederation Congress, state governments, and the new federal government; and evangelical movements of the early nineteenth century. The exhibit's broad focus is to explore efforts "to define the role of religious faith in public life

. . . not inconsistent with the revolutionary imperatives of the equality and freedom of all citizens." The website is useful for studying early American history, print culture, and the history of religion.

## 60. Rivers, Edens, Empires: Lewis and Clark and the Revealing of America
*Library of Congress*
http://www.loc.gov/exhibits/lewisandclark/lewisandclark.html

These 170 documents and artifacts interpret nineteenth-century westward exploration through three motivating forces present in President Thomas Jefferson's instructions to Lewis and Clark; a search for navigable rivers to span the continent; a quest for Edenic beauty and riches; and the competitive desire to acquire a continental empire. The range of materials is striking. In addition to maps, plans, and charts, the website offers images (sketches, watercolors, etchings, and engravings), texts (letters, diaries, speeches, newspapers, and books), and tools (surveying and medical instruments, cooking utensils, and armaments). The exhibit opens with an examination of the "imperial mentality" common to Virginia's aristocratic class in the late eighteenth century and then focuses on the Lewis and Clark journey. It ends with later expeditions of Zebulon Pike, Stephen H. Long, Charles Wilkes, and John Charles Frémont, and the mid-nineteenth century transcontinental railroad plan that supplanted the search for a water route.

## 61. Thomas Jefferson Digital Archive
*University of Virginia Library*
http://etext.lib.virginia.edu/jefferson

More than 1,700 texts written by or to Thomas Jefferson are available on this website, including correspondence, books, addresses, and public papers. Most of the texts are presented in transcribed, word-searchable format, but eighteen appear as color images of original manuscripts. The website also includes a biography of Jefferson written in 1834, eight years after his death. *The Jeffersonian Cyclopedia*, published in 1900, organizes more than 9,000 quotes according to theme and other categories. A collection of 2,700 excerpts from Jefferson's writings presents his political philosophy. A wealth of searchable bibliographic listings is provided, including two previously published volumes and thousands of additional bibliographic references. Also available are a dissertation on the construction of the Jefferson-designed University of Virginia (UVA), listings from the *Oxford English Dictionary* that show Jefferson's influence on English language usage, and four links to UVA exhibitions on Jefferson. These materials are valuable for studying Jefferson and the early republic.

## 62. Thomas Jefferson Papers
*Library of Congress, American Memory*
http://memory.loc.gov/ammem/mtjhtml/mtjhome.html

A remarkable collection, this website offers 27,000 documents, two-thirds of which are Jefferson's letters, notes, and drafts. Materials include official writings, such as statements and addresses, and material reflecting Jefferson's catholic intellectual, legal, scientific, and political interests. These range from records dealing with the history of Virginia to agriculture, anthropology, architecture, botany, literature, and travel. Correspondence covers the first fifty years of U.S. history, presenting an inside view of issues and events from Jefferson's position as delegate to the second Continental Congress (during which he drafted the Declaration of Independence) through his two presidential administrations. The website links to a Library of Congress exhibition on Jefferson and includes a timeline, selected quotations, and three essays. The documents are presented only as page images, and reading the handwriting can be slow.

### 63. Thomas Paine National Historical Association

*Kenneth Burchell, Thomas Paine National Historical Association*
http://www.thomaspaine.org

This website offers full-text versions of seven books and essays by Thomas Paine (1737–1809) in addition to five nineteenth- and early-twentieth-century biographies on his life and works. Materials include *Common Sense, The Rights of Man, The Age of Reason, The Crisis Papers,* "African Slavery in America," "Agrarian Justice," and "An Occasional Letter on the Female Sex." These texts are reproduced from *The Complete Writings of Thomas Paine,* a 1945 publication edited and annotated by historian Philip S. Foner. The website includes Foner's section introductions and his "Chronological Table of Thomas Paine's Writings." Unfortunately, the website also includes hundreds of broken links to additional essays and letters by Paine. The biographies presented provide works published from 1819 to 1925. The website also reprints Thomas Edison's 1925 essay, "The Philosophy of Thomas Paine," in which he attempted to reawaken interest in Paine.

## Expansion and Reform, 1801–1861

### 64. Abraham Lincoln Historical Digitization Project

*Drew VandeCreek, Northern Illinois University*
http://lincoln.lib.niu.edu

This wealth of historical materials, in a variety of formats, addresses Abraham Lincoln's years in Illinois (1831–1860) and Illinois history during the same period. The website provides more than 2,300 transcriptions of documents, including correspondence, speeches, treaties, and other official papers. Additional resources include sixty-three audio recordings of songs and 295 images of Lincoln, his family, friends, associates, and contemporaries, as well as Illinois towns, homes, and businesses. Materials are organized into eight thematic sections: *African American Experience and American Racial Attitudes; Economic Development and Labor; Frontier Settlement; Law and Society; Native American Relations; Politics; Religion and Culture;* and *Women's Experience and Gender Roles.* Each theme includes a background essay, relevant documents and images, video discussions by prominent historians, and narrated slide shows. *Lincoln's Biography* divides his life into eight segments with a summary and biographical text by scholars and includes a bibliography.

### 65. Abraham Lincoln Papers

*Library of Congress, American Memory; Lincoln Studies Center,
Knox College*

http://memory.loc.gov/ammem/alhtml/malhome.html

This website offers approximately 20,000 documents relating to President Abraham Lincoln's life and career. All of the materials are available as page images, and about half of them have been transcribed. Resources include correspondence, reports, pamphlets, and newspaper clippings. Although the documents date from 1833 to 1916, most material was written between 1850 and 1865, including drafts of the Emancipation Proclamation and Lincoln's second inaugural address. A chronological index offers names of correspondents and document titles. Special presentations on the Emancipation Proclamation and the Lincoln assassination provide introductions, timelines, and twenty-four images of related documents and engravings. Additional resources include sixteen photographs of the Lincolns and key political and military figures of Lincoln's presidency. This is an excellent resource for researching Lincoln's presidency and American politics prior to and during the Civil War.

### 66. Accessible Archives

*Accessible Archives*

http://www.accessible.com     $ $

This subscription-based website currently provides seven databases containing more than 176,000 articles from nineteenth-century newspapers, magazines, books, and genealogical records. Much of the material comes from Pennsylvania and other mid-Atlantic states. *Godey's Lady's Book* (1830–1880), one of the most popular nineteenth-century publications, furnished middle- and upper-class American women with fiction, fashion, illustrations, and editorials. The *Pennsylvania Gazette* (1728–1800), a Philadelphia newspaper, is described as "*The New York Times* of the eighteenth century." *The Civil War: A Newspaper Perspective* includes major articles from the *Charleston Mercury*, the *New York Herald*, and the *Richmond Enquirer*. *African American Newspapers: The Nineteenth Century* includes runs from six newspapers published in New York, Washington, D.C., and Toronto between 1827 and 1876. *American County Histories to 1900* provides sixty volumes covering the local history of New Jersey, Delaware, and Pennsylvania. *The Pennsylvania Genealogical Catalogue: Chester County 1809–1870* has been partially digitized, with 25,000 records available. *The Pennsylvania Newspaper Record: Delaware County 1819–1870*, also a work in progress, addresses industrialization in a rural area settled by Quaker farmers in the eighteenth century. All material within each database is keyword searchable, allowing users quick access to multiple perspectives on topics.

### 67. African Americans in Lancaster County

*Lancaster County Historical Society*

http://www.lancasterhistory.org/education/afam

The 100 documents available here address antebellum life in Lancaster County, Pennsylvania. Materials include photographs, letters, wills, tax records, maps, census records, court records, newspaper articles, inventories, and local government records regarding slavery in the county. There are nine activities and more than fifty documents for studying the underground railroad and the "Christiana Resistance" — the killing in 1851 of a Maryland farmer who came north to recover four escaped slaves, an event that achieved national significance. An exhibit explores middle-class African American life in the county, and a bibliography with more than 125 books, pamphlets, and articles. A timeline places the history of African Americans in Lancaster County into a national context. This small but diverse group of sources is valuable for researching African American history at the local level.

### 68. African American Women Writers of the Nineteenth Century
*Digital Schomburg: The New York Public Library*
http://digital.nypl.org/schomburg/writers_aa19

This website presents fifty-two published works by thirty-seven black women writers from the late eighteenth century through 1920. The full-text database offers works by late-eighteenth-century poet Phillis Wheatley, late-nineteenth-century essayist and novelist Alice Dunbar-Nelson, and Harriet Jacobs, a woman born into slavery who published her memoirs, *Incidents in the Life of a Slave Girl*, in the late nineteenth century. Users can browse by title, author, or type of work (fiction, poetry, biography and autobiography, and essays). Each browse category also contains a keyword search for subjects such as religion, family, and slavery. Brief biographies of the featured writers are available. This website is easy to use and is ideal for learning about African American history, women's history, and nineteenth-century American literature.

### 69. American Transcendentalism Web
*Ann Woodlief, Virginia Commonwealth University*
http://www.vcu.edu/engweb/transcendentalism

This website offers a comprehensive collection of texts by and about the major figures of American Transcendentalism, a New England intellectual movement that began in the mid-1830s and lasted into the late 1840s. The movement has had a much longer legacy, however, in American literature, philosophy, religion, and political and social reform. Some materials are available on the website; others are provided through links. Eleven major authors are featured — Ralph Waldo Emerson, Henry David Thoreau, Margaret Fuller, Reverend William Ellery Channing, his son William Ellery Channing, Theodore Parker, Amos Bronson Alcott, Jones Very, Christopher Cranch, Orestes Brownson, and Elizabeth Palmer Peabody. Texts are also retrievable according to themes and type of writing. Resources include more than 100 selections from *The Dial*, a journal created by the Transcendentalist Club in 1840, which lasted four years, and informative essays that provide a historic overview.

### 70. America's First Look into the Camera: Daguerreotype Portraits and Views, 1839–1864
*Library of Congress, American Memory*
http://memory.loc.gov/ammem/daghtml/daghome.html

This collection contains more than 725 early photographs, primarily daguerreotypes produced at the Mathew Brady studio. The Brady images include portraits of prominent public figures, such as President James K. Polk, Thomas Hart Benton, Thomas Cole, Horace Greeley, and the earliest known images of President and Mrs. Abraham Lincoln. In addition, the website presents daguerreotypes by African American photographers, architectural views taken around Washington, D.C., and Baltimore, street scenes of Philadelphia, early portraits by Robert Cornelius, and copies of painted portraits. A short introduction to the daguerreotype medium and a "Timeline of the Daguerrian Era" provide context for the images. A special presentation, "Mirror Images: Daguerreotypes at the Library of Congress," includes photographs from the American Colonization Society, occupational daguerreotypes, portraits, and architectural views. Useful for studying nineteenth-century photography and visual culture, as well as for viewing some of the earliest American photographs.

### 71. Chickasaw Historical Research Page
*K. M. Armstrong*
http://www.flash.net/~kma

This website is dedicated to making documents available concerning the Chickasaw Indian Nation — originally located in the South but removed to Oklahoma Territory in the 1830s. Created by a member of the Chickasaw Indian Nation, this website contains more than 130 letters written by, to, or about the Chickasaw between 1792 and 1849; the texts of more than thirty treaties; and twenty-five additional documents

1846 photograph of the U.S. Capitol at *America's First Look into the Camera* [70].
*(Library of Congress)*

such as tribal rolls, census information, government records, and Bible entries. A linked website by the same author, *Chickasaw Nation, Indian Territory: 1837–1907* (**http://www.rootsweb.com/~itchicka**), contains a 650-word essay on Chickasaw Nation history and links to more than fifteen websites pertaining to the Chickasaw and American Indian subjects.

### 72. Dred Scott Case
*Washington University Libraries*
http://library.wustl.edu/vlib/dredscott

Facsimiles and transcriptions of eighty-five recently preserved legal documents relating to the eleven-year Dred Scott Case are provided on this website. The case began in 1846 when slaves Dred and Harriet Scott sued for their freedom, basing their argument on the fact that they had lived a number of years in nonslave territories. The case ended with the landmark U.S. Supreme Court decision of 1857, which denied citizenship to Scott and thus the right to sue in federal court. The Court also ruled that Scott had never been free and that Congress did not have the right to prohibit slavery in the territories. The decision sparked increased sectional tensions leading to the Civil War. The website also provides a chronology and links to 281 "Freedom Suits" — legal petitions for freedom filed by or on behalf of slaves — in St. Louis courts from 1814 to 1860.

### 73. Edgar Allan Poe
*Edgar Allan Poe Society of Baltimore*
http://www.eapoe.org

This rich collection offers annotated versions of most of the material published by Edgar Allan Poe during his lifetime (1809–1849), including at least one example of all surviving poems and tales and in many cases multiple versions. Materials include selections of Poe's literary reviews and essays on a variety of subjects, such as aesthetics, dreams, etiquette, American novels, poetry, and magazine literature. Autobiographical writings, hundreds of letters, and miscellaneous documents, including a bill of sale for a slave, are also available. The website offers annotated chronologies of Poe's life and time in Baltimore as well as informative essays on selected topics, such as speculations concerning his death. There are general and topic-related bibliographies, issues of the *Poe Newsletter* from 1968 to 1970 and *Poe Studies* from 1971 to 1979, two contemporary reviews of his work, and one death notice. Two recent scholarly articles round out the holdings. There is an abundance of material for studying Poe and the literary scene in antebellum America.

### 74. Freedom Bound: The Underground Railroad in Lycoming County, Pennsylvania
*Lynn Estomin, Lycoming College*
www.lycoming.edu/underground

This Flash-based website investigates the Underground Railroad in Lycoming County, Pennsylvania. Users go to a map of the environs near Williamsport dotted with thirteen relevant locations. Clicking on a location brings up images and streaming audio testimony from oral historian Mamie Sweeting Diggs. Diggs details the site's significance using stories passed down from her great grandfather, Daniel

Hughes, an agent and conductor on the railroad. A river raftsman, Hughes floated logs down the Susquehanna River to Maryland and then returned, leading slaves on foot along a mountain trail. Slaves hid in warehouses, caves, and Hughes's own home. Helped by Hughes and his cohorts, the slaves headed for nearby Freedom Road and traveled to Canada by foot or train. More than fifty photographs and prints document the places where the story took place. Diggs relates four additional stories from Hughes.

### 75. *Godey's Lady's Book* Online
*Electronic Historical Publications, University of Rochester*
http://www.history.rochester.edu/godeys

One of the most popular nineteenth-century publications, *Godey's Lady's Book* furnished middle- and upper-class American women with fiction, fashion, illustrations, and editorials from 1830 through 1898. This website provides material from five 1850 issues of the publication. Each issue includes poetry, engravings, and articles by major writers such as Oliver Wendell Holmes, Henry Wadsworth Longfellow, and Sarah Joseph Hale, as well as a section on Victorian fashion. Materials include more than fifty high-resolution pictures. This is a valuable resource for learning about Victorian popular culture, print culture, and middle-class women. The University of Vermont offers a similar website with three full issues from 1855 and a partial issue from 1852 (http://www.uvm.edu:80/~hag/godey). The full run of the magazine may be found in the subscription service *Accessible Archives* [66].

### 76. Helios: The Smithsonian American Art Museum Photography Collection
*Smithsonian American Art Museum*
http://AmericanArt.si.edu/helios

More than 300 photographs are presented on this website in three exhibits. *The First Century of American Photographs* features more than 175 nineteenth- and early-twentieth-century daguerreotypes and photographs, including Civil War images, western landscapes, and people at work and play from 1839 to 1939. Scholars discuss specific images in audio clips, focusing on commerce and industry, identity, and the picturesque. *Between Home and Heaven* offers a collection of ninety recent landscape photographs taken throughout the United States. *American Daguerreotypes* tours the history of daguerreotype, presenting twelve portraits, landscapes, and occupationals (photographs of people taken with tools of their occupation), along with excerpts from the 1995 book *Secrets of the Dark: The Art of American Daguerreotypes*. There are twelve audio clips of scholars discussing the history and art of daguerreotype. This website provides illuminating images for studying early American photography and its role in American cultural history.

### 77. James Fenimore Cooper Society
*Hugh MacDougall, The James Fenimore Cooper Society*
http://external.oneonta.edu/cooper

Hard-to-find works by the great American writer James Fenimore Cooper (1789–1851) and his eldest daughter, Susan Fenimore Cooper (1813–1894), a writer and naturalist, are available here. Additional materials, including reference documents, articles, and papers on Cooper are well indexed. In total, the website provides more than 300 texts. Nine full works by Cooper, annotated by transcriber Hugh MacDougall, are offered, including short stories, a novel, social satires, a surviving scene from Cooper's only play, and a never-completed history of New York. The website includes plot summaries for all of Cooper's thirty-two novels and four nineteenth-century spoofs and parodies of Cooper's works. In addition, Susan Cooper's introductions to twenty-five of her father's novels are provided along with twelve of her writings, including a novel, stories for children, and an argument against female suffrage. This is a good source for lesser-known works by Cooper and his daughter as well as for recent studies that discuss Cooper's historical significance.

### 78. Lester S. Levy Collection of Sheet Music
*Milton S. Eisenhower Library, Johns Hopkins University*
http://levysheetmusic.mse.jhu.edu

Scanned images of more than 18,000 pieces of sheet music, including covers, published prior to 1923 are presented on this website. The collection, compiled by

The United Nations Anthem from *Lester S. Levy Collection of Sheet Music* [78].
*(The Lester S. Levy Collection, The Sheridan Libraries of The Johns Hopkins University)*

an American musicologist, covers the period from 1780 to 1980 but focuses on nineteenth-century popular music, especially songs relating to military conflicts, presidents, romance, and transportation, and songs from the minstrel stage. Users may search for songs on hundreds of topics, such as drinking, smoking, fraternal orders, the circus, and death, or they may look for composers, song titles, or other catalog record data. Descriptions by the collector of significant songs in thirty-eight topical categories are also available. These materials are useful for studying nineteenth- and early-twentieth-century popular culture, especially depictions of ethnicity, gender, and race.

### 79. Lewis and Clark: The Journey of the Corps of Discovery
*PBS Online*
http://www.pbs.org/lewisandclark

This is a PBS companion website for the film *The Journey of the Corps of Discovery* by Ken Burns. The website contains brief biographies of members of the expedition and historical sketches of the American Indian tribes encountered by Lewis and Clark. Materials also include a semi-searchable selection of transcribed journal excerpts from six expedition members totaling 140,000 words and more than 800 minutes of unedited interviews with scholars and other specialists. An interactive trail map through eleven states includes links to journal entries and information on Indian history. The website also provides an annotated timeline, more than thirty links to related websites, a bibliography, and discussions with film-maker Ken Burns.

### 80. "Liberty Rhetoric" and Nineteenth-Century American Women
*Catherine Lavender, College of Staten Island*
http://www.library.csi.cuny.edu/dept/americanstudies/
lavender/liberty.html

This website offers three case studies on nineteenth-century women's use of "liberty rhetoric"—a way of speaking about the relationship between the citizen and the state—to argue for their own liberties. The first section offers seven documents, two poems, and three images depicting origins of liberty rhetoric in the Revolutionary tradition. The second provides nine documents and five images tracing the operations of textile mills in Lowell, Massachusetts, and the liberty rhetoric that female mill workers used during strikes in 1834 and 1836. This section also offers ten images of Lowell and the lives of young women who flocked to the mill town to earn money and experience some measure of autonomy. The third section provides the text of the 1848 Declaration of Sentiments and compares it to the Declaration of Independence as an expression of liberty rhetoric. There are five links to related websites. These materials are valuable for learning about women, language, and reform movements.

### 81. North American Slave Narratives, Beginnings to 1920
*William Andrews, University of North Carolina at Chapel Hill*
http://docsouth.unc.edu/neh/neh.html

This collection offers 230 full-text documents on the lives of American slaves, including all known published slave narratives and many published biographies of slaves. Documents are available in HTML and SGML/TEI file formats and are accessible through alphabetical and chronological listings. Users can also view images of the covers, spines, title pages, and versos of title pages. The documents have been indexed by subject, but searches return materials in additional collections. An introductory essay by Professor Andrews is available. These materials are very valuable for studying American slavery, the South, African American culture, and slave narratives.

### 82. Oregon Trail
*Mike Trinklein and Steve Boettcher, Idaho State University*
http://www.isu.edu/~trinmich/Oregontrail.html

Created as a companion to the PBS documentary of the same name, this website details the history of the Oregon Trail and experiences of settlers who used it to migrate west beginning in the early 1840s. Archival materials include full texts of seven diaries, two letters, nine memoirs, and six complete books about journeys along the Oregon Trail from such authors as Francis Parkman, John Charles Frémont, and Horace Greeley. A 5,000-word essay on the trail and travelers' experiences includes links to archived texts and to approximately thirty video interviews with historians who consulted on the documentary. Access to thirty-two historic

Illustration from *North American Slave Narratives, Beginnings to 1920* [81].
*(Documenting the American South, The University of North Carolina at Chapel Hill Libraries, North Carolina Collection)*

websites offers links to additional material. The website is easy to navigate and has a keyword search feature, but a fuller picture of the topic requires the use of library resources.

### 83. Samuel J. May Anti-Slavery Collection
*Cornell University Library*
http://www.library.cornell.edu/mayantislavery

This is one of the richest collections of antislavery and Civil War materials in the world. Reverend Samuel J. May, an American abolitionist, donated his collection of antislavery materials to the Cornell Library in 1870. Following May's lead, other abolitionists in the United States and Great Britain contributed materials. The collection now consists of more than 10,000 pamphlets, leaflets, broadsides, local antislavery society newsletters, sermons, essays, and arguments for and against slavery. Materials date from 1773 to 1934 and cover slavery in the United States and the West Indies, the slave trade, and emancipation. More than 300,000 pages are available for full-text searching. Accompanying the documents are twelve links to other collections. This is an important resource for studying slavery and abolition.

## 84. Slave Movement during the Eighteenth and Nineteenth Centuries

*Data and Program Library Service, University of Wisconsin Madison*
http://dpls.dacc.wisc.edu/slavedata

Downloadable raw data and documentation on eleven topics related to the eighteenth- and nineteenth-century slave trade are available on this website. Materials include records of slave ship movement between Africa and the Americas from 1817 to 1843, the eighteenth-century Virginia slave trade, slave trade to Jamaica from 1782 to 1788 and 1805 to 1808, slave ships of eighteenth-century France, and the English slave trade from 1791 to 1799. Data sets contain information such as ports of departure and arrival, vessel and owner information, and numbers and origins of slaves carried. Each data set includes a 250-word description explaining bibliographic information, file inventory, and methodology, as well as a codebook that guides users in reading the data. Data are provided without analysis, and the website carries a warning that data analysis is time-consuming work requiring specialized software. The materials, though, offer a very valuable resource on the history of slavery and the slave trade.

## 85. Slaves and the Courts, 1740–1860

*Library of Congress, American Memory*
http://memory.loc.gov/ammem/sthtml/sthome.html

More than 100 published materials on legal aspects of slavery are available on this website. These include 8,700 pages of court decisions and arguments, reports, proceedings, journals, and letters. Most of the pamphlets and books pertain to American cases in the nineteenth century. Additional documents address the slave trade, slave codes, the Fugitive Slave Law, and slave insurrections as well as presenting courtroom proceedings from famous trials such as the eighteenth-century *Somerset* v. *Stewart* case in England, the *Amistad* case, the Denmark Vesey conspiracy trial, and trials of noted abolitionists John Brown and William Lloyd Garrison. A special presentation discusses the slave code in the District of Columbia. Searchable by keyword, subject, author, and title, this website is valuable for studying legal history, African American history, and nineteenth-century American history.

## 86. Sunday School Books: Shaping the Values of Youth in Nineteenth-Century America

*Library of Congress, American Memory; Michigan State*
*University Libraries; Central Michigan University*
http://memory.loc.gov/ammem/award99/miemhtml/svyhome.html

These full-text transcriptions and page images of 163 "Sunday school books" address religious instruction for youth published in the United States between 1815 and 1865. Materials include texts used by Methodists, Baptists, Mormons, and other denominations and are searchable by subject, author, title, and keyword. Books are categorized according to nine types — *Advice Books, Moral Tales*; *Animals, Natural History*; *Child Labor, Orphans, Poverty*; *Death, Dying, Illness*; *Holidays*; *Immigrants*; *Slavery, African Americans, Native Americans*; *Temperance, Tobacco*; and *Travel, Missionaries*. There are sixty-two author biographies and an essay on Sunday school books. These are valuable materials for studying antebellum culture, American religious history, print culture, and education.

## 87. Trails to Utah and the Pacific: Diaries and Letters, 1846–1869

*Library of Congress, American Memory; Brigham Young University;*
*Utah Academic Library Consortium*

http://memory.loc.gov/ammem/award99/upbhtml/overhome.html

Diaries documenting the westward treks of forty-five men and four women during the period of the California gold rush and rise of Mormonism are presented on this website. Although most of these travelers took either the California or the Mormon trail, a few diaries provide accounts describing life on trails to Oregon and Montana. The diaries are complemented by eighty-two photographs and illustrations in addition to forty-three maps, including an interactive map displaying trails, cities, rivers, and landmarks. There are seven published guides, two essays on the Mormon and California trails, brief biographies of most of the diarists, and a list of suggested readings. This is an excellent collection of materials that documents forty-nine individual perspectives on a movement that encompassed an estimated 500,000 people.

## 88. Women in America: 1820 to 1842

*Mary Halnon, University of Virginia*

http://xroads.virginia.edu/~HYPER/DETOC/FEM

This website presents excerpts of eighteen texts that discuss the status of women in America between 1820 and 1842. Texts were written by travelers from Ireland, Germany, Scotland, England, France, and America, and authors include Charles Dickens, Alexis de Tocqueville, Frances Trollope, Harriet Martineau, Frederick Marryat, Charles Lyell, Michel Chevalier, and James Fenimore Cooper. The thirteen topics include marriage and courtship, work, law and government, education, race, arts and entertainment, fashion, travel, asylums and penitentiaries, wilderness, health, Indians, and religion. The website proposes to ascertain the accuracy of "the picture of women in [Tocqueville's] *Democracy in America*" by comparing it with contemporary works and includes a link to the complete text of *Democracy in America*, biographical essays on each writer, and a twenty-item bibliography.

## 89. Women's History: The 1850 Worcester Convention

*Worcester Women's History Project, Assumption College*

http://www.assumption.edu/wwhp/hr.html

To commemorate the 150th anniversary of the First National Women's Rights Convention, held in 1850 in Worcester, Massachusetts, this website provides an archive of relevant documents. Materials include eight speeches, fifteen newspaper accounts, fourteen letters, and selected items from the proceedings. Also available are three speeches from the 1851 convention and resources concerning the nineteenth-century woman's movement more broadly. These include diary entries, government reports, tracts for and against suffrage, poems from *Godey's Lady's Book*, and the full text of several books, such as *The Lady's Guide to Perfect Gentility* (1856). The website presents essays about, and selections by, advocates for women's rights, such as Jane Grey Swisshelm and Caroline Wells Healy Dall. Comprehensive with regard to the 1850 convention, the website is also useful for providing resources on the mid-nineteenth-century women's rights movement.

# Civil War and Reconstruction, 1850–1877

### 90. Born in Slavery: Slave Narratives from the Federal Writers' Project, 1936–1938

*Library of Congress, American Memory*

http://lcweb2.loc.gov/ammem/snhtml/snhome.html

More than 2,300 firsthand accounts of slavery and 500 black and white photographs of former slaves are available here. These materials were collected in the 1930s by the Federal Writers' Project of the Works Project Administration, a Roosevelt administration New Deal bureau. Each slave narrative transcript is accompanied by notes including the name of the narrator, place and date of the interview, interviewer's name, length of transcript, and catalog information. Each photograph has similar notes. Browse photographs and narratives by keyword, subject, and narrator. An introductory essay discusses the significance of slave narratives and includes a selection of excerpts from eight narratives along with photographs of the former slaves. This is a rich resource for exploring slavery, historical memory, and New Deal efforts to document America's past.

### 91. Central Pacific Railroad Photographic History Museum

*Central Pacific Railroad Museum*

http://cprr.org

This large collection of materials emphasizes the first transcontinental railroad, the Central Pacific, completed in 1869, and rail travel in general. The website offers more than 2,000 photographs and images, including stereographs by Alfred Hart and Eadweard Muybridge; engravings and illustrations from magazines, travel brochures, and journals; and more than 400 railroad and travel maps. Also included are more than sixty links to images and transcriptions of documents dealing with the construction and operation of the railroad, including government reports, travel accounts and diaries, magazine and journal articles, travel guides, and railroad schedules. A section documents Chinese American contributions to the transcontinental railroad, with scholarly articles, two links to *Harper's Weekly* articles and illustrations, a bibliography of fifteen scholarly works, and links to more than twenty related websites. Timelines help contextualize the material. Some materials load slowly.

### 92. Civil War Treasures from the New-York Historical Society

*Library of Congress, American Memory; New-York Historical Society*

http://memory.loc.gov/ammem/ndlpcoop/nhihtml/cwnyhshome.html

More than 1,500 items pertaining to the Civil War are available on this website, such as letters, newspapers, photographs, sketches, etchings, and posters. Manuscript materials include items from the papers of social reformer William Oland Bourne, a newspaper created by Confederate prisoners, three letters by Walt Whitman, and thirty-two letters by a nurse at a federal prison camp hospital. The website contains sketches dealing with the New York City draft riot of 1863; drawings of army life by artists working for *Frank Leslie's Illustrated Newspaper*, a Confederate prisoner's sketchbook; 731 stereographs; 70 albumen photographs; approximately 500 envelopes with decorative materials; twenty-nine caricatures by a German immigrant in Baltimore sympathetic to the Confederacy; and 304 posters, most of which were used for recruiting purposes. This website is valuable for exploring the Civil War and visual images during wartime.

### 93. Freedmen and Southern Society Project
*Freedmen and Southern Society Project*
http://www.history.umd.edu/Freedmen

These forty-four documents focus on the emancipation of African American slaves between 1861 and 1865. Texts include a letter by General William T. Sherman explaining why he refused to return fugitive slaves to their owners; an 1864 letter from a Maryland slave to President Abraham Lincoln asking for clarification of her legal status; and a description by a Union general of a bloody battle at Milliken's Bend, Louisiana, where a brigade of black soldiers fought. Documents from federal and Confederate governments appear as links within an authoritative chronology of events leading to emancipation. The transcribed documents are accompanied by sentence-long annotations. This website is part of a larger effort underway by the Freedmen and Southern Society Project to publish the multivolume *Freedom: A Documentary History of Emancipation, 1861–1867*. Although relatively small, the website provides firsthand accounts of emancipation along with well-chosen contextual documents.

### 94. Freedmen's Bureau Online
*Christine's Genealogy Websites*
http://www.freedmensbureau.com

The Bureau of Refugees, Freedmen, and Abandoned Lands, also known as the Freedmen's Bureau, was established by the War Department in 1865 to supervise all relief and education activities for refugees and freedmen after the Civil War. The Bureau was responsible for issuing rations, clothing, and medicine, and had custody of confiscated lands in the former Confederate states and other designated territories. This website contains an extensive collection of Freedmen's Bureau records and reports. Included are more than 100 transcriptions of reports on murders, riots, and "outrages" (any criminal offense) that occurred in the former Confederate states from 1865 to 1868; roughly thirty links to records and indexes of labor contracts between freedmen and planters between 1865 and 1872; six links to marriage records of freedmen from 1861 to 1872; and more than 100 miscellaneous state record items concerning freedmen. The website is ideal for researching Reconstruction in the South and African American labor, cultural, and family history.

### 95. *HarpWeek:* Explore History
*HarpWeek, LLC*
http://www.harpweek.com

Attached to the larger *HarpWeek* subscription website [118], this collection of thirteen exhibits presents free access to a wealth of texts and images on a variety of subjects dealing with nineteenth-century American history. Each section provides illustrations, articles, editorials, and overviews. Materials include four exhibits on politics and elections: *The Presidential Elections—1860–1912; American Political Prints, 1766–1876; The Impeachment of Andrew Johnson;* and *Hayes vs. Tilden.* Two exhibits deal with race and ethnicity: *Toward Racial Equality: "Harper's Weekly" Reports on Black America, 1857–1874* and *The Chinese American Experience: 1857–1892.* Three exhibits offer material on business and consumer culture: *Nineteenth-Century Advertising History; Business Machines, 1857–1912;* and *Coffin Nails: The Tobacco Controversy in the Nineteenth Century. Additional exhibits include: The American West; A Sampler of Civil War Literature; Russian-American Relations, 1863–1905;* and *The World of Thomas Nast.* This is a valuable website for studying nineteenth-century print culture and coverage of subjects of national concern.

## 96. Historical New York Times Project — The Civil War Years, 1860–1866
*University Library, Carnegie Mellon University*
http://www.nyt.ulib.org

Designed to provide access to the *New York Times* for the Civil War years, this website includes reproductions of all pages from the 1860s and from the years 1900 to 1907. For the war years, more than eighty significant articles are arranged chronologically by year and in the following topics: battles, military, politics, relations among the States, and social issues. These articles deal with Lincoln's election, inauguration, and assassination, press censorship, abolition of slavery, formation of the Confederate States of America, and Sherman's March to the Sea, among other topics. In addition, users can select any page for any issue published during the decade. Full-text access to the newspaper's complete run is available through the subscription service *ProQuest* [33].

## 97. Lost Museum
*ASHP/CML and New Media Lab, CUNY*
http://www.lostmuseum.cuny.edu

This website re-creates P. T. Barnum's American Museum. The museum burned down in mysterious circumstances in 1865 after enjoying nearly a quarter century of patronage. The original museum tried both to entertain and to educate with exhibits on natural history, American history, and reform efforts along with attractions of a sensational nature. With the exception of African Americans, who were barred until the Civil War, New Yorkers of diverse ethnic, gender, and class identities mingled in the museum's shared cultural space. Visitors may explore interactive three-dimensional re-creations of sixteen original Barnum exhibits or an archive of images, documents, accounts, and essays. Exhibits include the Fejee mermaid; Joice Heth, a former slave advertised as George Washington's nursemaid; "Swedish Nightingale" Jenny Lind; John Brown; Jefferson Davis; the Lincoln assassination; the Civil War in New York; and phrenology. The website allows visitors to immerse themselves in the popular culture of Barnum's era.

### 98. Making of America
*University of Michigan*
http://moa.umdl.umich.edu

*Cornell University*
http://cdl.library.cornell.edu/moa

Together, these two websites provide more than 1.5 million pages of text in a collaborative effort to digitize more than 11,000 volumes and 100,000 journal articles from the nineteenth century. The websites present full-text access to thirty-two journals, including literary and political magazines such as *Atlantic Monthly* and *Harper's New Monthly Magazine*. The list includes specialized journals as well, such as *Scientific American, Manufacturer and Builder, Ladies Repository*, and *American Missionary*. The websites also offer an abundance of novels and monographs. A recent addition provides 149 volumes on New York City, some from the early twentieth century. At present, the two collections remain separate and must be searched individually. The institutions plan to integrate their websites, however, and to include material from other major research libraries. Access to many *Making of America* texts also is available through the Library of Congress's American Memory website *The Nineteenth Century in Print* (http://memory.loc.gov/ammem/ndlpcoop/moahtml/ncphome.html).

### 99. Selected Civil War Photographs
*Library of Congress, American Memory*
http://memory.loc.gov/ammem/cwphtml/cwphome.html

This collection offers 1,118 photographs depicting Civil War military personnel, preparations for battle, and the aftermath of battles in the main eastern theater and in the West. Photographs also cover U.S. navy and Atlantic seaborne expeditions against the Confederacy, portraits of Confederate and Union officers and enlisted men, and photographs of Washington, D.C., during the war. Most images were created under the supervision of photographer Mathew B. Brady. Additional photographs were made by Alexander Gardner after leaving Brady's employment to start his own business. The presentation "Time Line of the Civil War" places images in historical context. "Does the Camera Ever Lie?" demonstrates the constructed nature of images, showing that photographers sometimes rearranged elements of their images to achieve a more controlled effect. This website is useful for studying nineteenth-century American photography and Civil War history.

### 100. *Uncle Tom's Cabin* and American Culture
*Stephen Railton, University of Virginia*
http://jefferson.village.virginia.edu/utc

This well-designed, comprehensive website explores Harriet Beecher Stowe's *Uncle Tom's Cabin* "as an American cultural phenomenon." *Pre Texts, 1830–1852* provides dozens of texts, songs, and images from the various genres Stowe drew upon: Christian texts, sentimental culture, antislavery texts, and minstrel shows. The section on the novel includes Stowe's preface, multiple versions of the text, playable songs from the novel, and Stowe's defense against criticism. A third section focuses on responses from 1852 to 1930, including twelve reviews, more than 100 articles

Early war photography from *Selected Civil War Photographs* [99].
*(Library of Congress)*

and notes, as well as twenty responses from African Americans and dozens from pro-slavery adherents. *Other Media* explores theatrical versions, children's books, songs, and games. Three interpretive exhibits challenge users to investigate how slavery and race were defined and redefined as well as how the character of Topsy was created and re-created to assume a range of political and social meanings. This excellent resource examines popular culture within historical contexts.

### 101. Valley of the Shadow: Two Communities in the American Civil War
*Virginia Center for Digital History, University of Virginia*
http://valley.vcdh.virginia.edu

A massive, searchable archive compares two Shenandoah Valley counties during the Civil War period — Augusta County, Virginia, and Franklin County, Pennsylvania. These two counties were divided by 200 miles and the institution of slavery. Thousands of pages of maps, images, letters, diaries, and newspapers, in addition to church, agricultural, military, and public records, provide data, experiences, and perspectives from the eve of the war until its aftermath. The website furnishes time-lines, bibliographies, and other materials intended to foster research and allow students to "explore every dimension of the conflict." The website includes a section on

Early edition illustrations from
*"Uncle Tom's Cabin" and
American Culture* [100].
*(Stephen Railton, University of
Virginia)*

John Brown (http://jefferson.village.virginia.edu/jbrown/master.html) and one entitled *Memory of the War*, presenting postwar writings on battles, the lives of soldiers,
reunions, obituaries and tributes, and politics.

### 102. Wright American Fiction, 1851–1875

*Committee on Institutional Cooperation; Indiana University
Digital Library Program*

http://www.letrs.indiana.edu/web/w/wright2

An ambitious attempt to digitize "every novel published in the United States from
1851 to 1875," this collection of texts is a work-in-progress. At present, the website
offers close to 3,000 texts by 1,394 authors. Of these, 778 have been fully edited and
SGML encoded so that users may access chapter and story divisions through table
of contents hyperlinks. The remaining texts can be read either as facsimiles of original pages or in unedited transcriptions. The ability to perform single word and
phrase searches on all material in the database — whether fully encoded or not — is
powerful. This is a valuable resource for studying American literature and popular
culture of the nineteenth century.

## Development of the Industrial United States, 1870–1900

### 103. African American Perspectives: Pamphlets from the Daniel A. P. Murray Collection, 1818–1907

*Library of Congress, American Memory*

http://memory.loc.gov/ammem/aap/aaphome.html

This collection presents 350 African American pamphlets and documents, most produced between 1875 and 1900. The works include sermons, organization reports,

college catalogs, graduation orations, slave narratives, congressional speeches, poetry, and play scripts. Topics cover segregation, voting rights, violence against African Americans, and the colonization movement. Authors include Frederick Douglass, Booker T. Washington, Ida B. Wells-Barnett, Benjamin W. Arnett, Alexander Crummel, and Emanuel Love. Each pamphlet is accompanied by publication information and a short description of content. The website also offers a timeline of African American history from 1852 to 1925 and reproductions of original documents and illustrations. A special presentation called "The Progress of a People" re-creates a meeting of the National Afro-American Council in December 1898. This is a rich resource for studying nineteenth- and early-twentieth-century African American leaders and representatives of African American religious, civic, and social organizations.

### 104. Alexander Graham Bell Family Papers

*Library of Congress, American Memory*
http://memory.loc.gov/ammem/bellhtml/bellhome.html

This website presents 4,650 items from the papers of telephone inventor Alexander Graham Bell (1847–1922). Materials include family papers, general correspondence, and laboratory notebooks from 1891 to 1893 and from 1910, scientific notebooks, blueprints, journals, articles, lectures, and photographs. Writings cover a multitude of subjects, including the telephone, deaf education, experiments with aeronautics, and other inventions. There are more than 100 letters to and from Helen Keller, family correspondence, and material on life in Washington, D.C. — then a center for scientific research — and Nova Scotia, where Bell had a summer home and conducted experiments. The website also presents ten "collection highlights," including notebook pages documenting his first success with the telephone; essays on Bell's career and on the telephone; an annotated timeline; a bibliography with nineteen titles; and a list of ten related websites. This website is useful for studying the history of communications, the late-nineteenth-century and early-twentieth-century scientific community, and developments in deaf education.

### 105. American Indians of the Pacific Northwest

*Library of Congress, American Memory; University of Washington Libraries*
http://memory.loc.gov/ammem/award98/wauhtml/aipnhome.html

This archive includes more than 2,300 photographs and 7,700 pages of text illustrating the everyday lives of American Indians in the coastal and plateau regions of the Pacific Northwest. Materials illustrate housing, clothing, crafts, transportation, education, employment, and other aspects of everyday life among American Indians in this region. Most of the photographs were taken before 1920. Texts include more than 3,800 pages from the annual reports of the Commissioner of Indian Affairs to the Secretary of the Interior from 1851 through 1908; eighty-nine *Pacific Northwest Quarterly* articles from 1906 to 1998; and twenty-three titles in the University of Washington *Publications in Anthropology* series. The website also offers fourteen maps and ten lengthy essays authored by anthropologists on specific tribal groups and cross-cultural topics. Material is searchable by keyword and can be browsed by subject, geographic location, and author/photographer.

Documentary photograph from
*American Indians of the Pacific
Northwest* [105].
*(Library of Congress)*

### 106. Booker T. Washington Papers
*University of Illinois Press, History Cooperative*
http://www.historycooperative.org/btw

Booker T. Washington, born a slave in Virginia, became a central figure in the quest for education and equality for African Americans after the Civil War. In 1881, he founded the Tuskegee Normal and Industrial Institute in Alabama and became an influential educator and leader. Washington promoted vocational education for African Americans and was criticized for cultivating white approval. The complete fourteen-volume set of Washington's Papers is available on this website, including the well-known "Atlanta Compromise Address" and his autobiography *Up from Slavery*. Texts include books, articles, speeches, and correspondence covering the years 1860 to 1915 and are word searchable. The website also includes hundreds of photographs and illustrations collected into six volumes to accompany the texts. This is an excellent resource for studying Booker T. Washington.

### 107. "California as I Saw It": First-Person Narratives of California's Early Years, 1849–1900
*Library of Congress, American Memory*
http://memory.loc.gov/ammem/cbhtml/cbhome.html

The 190 works presented on this website — approximately 40,000 written pages and more than 3,000 illustrations — provide eyewitness accounts covering California history from the gold rush through the end of the nineteenth century. Most authors represented are white, educated, male, and American, including reporters detailing gold rush incidents and visitors from the 1880s attracted to a highly publicized, romantic vision of California life. The narratives, in the form of diaries, descriptions, guidebooks, and subsequent reminiscences, portray encounters with those living in California, the impact of mining, ranching, agriculture, and urban development, the growth of cities, and California's unique place in American culture. A special presentation recounts early California history, and a discussion of the collection's strengths and weaknesses provides useful context for the first-person accounts.

## 108. Centennial Exhibition, Philadelphia 1876

*Free Library of Philadelphia*
http://libwww.library.phila.gov/CenCol

The International Exhibition of Arts, Manufactures, and Products of the Soil and Mine, unofficially known as the Centennial Exhibition, was held in Philadelphia in 1876 and was attended by 9 million people. This website presents more than 1,500 photographs — mostly silver albumen prints — from the Exhibition, searchable by keyword or subject. *Exhibition Facts* provides statistics, a summary of the fair's significance, quotes from public figures, photographs of buildings erected by foreign nations, and images of sheet music. A timeline traces the fair's life span from the 1871 act of Congress that created its planning commission to the removal of exhibits in December 1876. A bibliography lists more than 150 related works. *Tours* features an interactive map of the fairgrounds. *Centennial Schoolhouse* offers activities for students, including excerpts from a seventeen-year-old girl's diary. This website provides revealing images of the event that introduced "America as a new industrial world power."

## 109. Chicago Anarchists on Trial: Evidence from the Haymarket Affair, 1886–1887

*Library of Congress, American Memory; Chicago Historical Society*
http://memory.loc.gov/ammem/award98/ichihtml/hayhome.html

This collection of documents — roughly 3,800 pages of court proceedings — concerns the Haymarket Affair. This watershed event in the history of American radicalism led to the first "Red Scare" in America. Materials include autobiographies of two of the eight anarchists tried for conspiracy in the murder of seven Chicago police officers. The officers died after a bomb exploded at an anarchist meeting in May 1886, the day after two workers died in a struggle between police and locked-out union members at the McCormick Reaper factory. Four defendants were executed, despite lack of evidence connecting them to the bombing. The website presents approximately 125 newspaper clippings, sixty photographs, thirteen letters, nine broadsides, and images of more than twenty artifacts. A linked exhibition, *The Dramas of Haymarket*, furnishes a historical narrative and contextual interpretation. This website is valuable for the study of late nineteenth-century American radicalism, law enforcement, and political climate.

## 110. Coal Mining in the Gilded Age and Progressive Era

*Ohio State University Department of History*
http://www.cohums.ohio-state.edu/history/projects/
Lessons_US/Gilded_Age/Coal_Mining

This collection about coal mining in the nineteenth century consists of seventeen separate pages about coal mining, mining disasters, strikes, and life in coal-mining communities. Most pages offer primary sources created between 1869 and 1904, such as an essay on the dangers of coal mining, an account of an 1869 cave-in, and Stephen Crane's 1894 article, "In the Depths of a Coal Mine." Additional materials include eight photographs of coal miners from 1904, twelve texts on an anthracite coal operators' strike in 1902 called by the United Mine Workers of America, and a thirty-page account of labor violence written by a Pinkerton agent in 1894.

### 111. Core Historical Literature of Agriculture
*Albert R. Mann Library, Cornell University*
http://chla.library.cornell.edu

Currently this website presents full-text, word-searchable facsimiles of 846 monographs related to agriculture published in the United States between 1847 and 1967. The materials are selected from the seven-volume series *The Literature of the Agricultural Sciences*. Fields of study covered include agricultural economics, agricultural engineering, animal science, forestry, nutrition, rural sociology, and soil science. Types of materials include memoirs and transactions of early agricultural societies, newspapers, almanacs, agricultural periodicals, governmental publications, and archives of families, communities, and corporations. Users can search by author, title, subject, or keyword, then access a text's title page, table of contents, index, or pages. This site is valuable for studying the profound social, cultural, and economic effects of shifts in the history of American farming.

### 112. David Rumsey Historical Map Collection
*David Rumsey, Cartography Associates*
http://www.davidrumsey.com

This private collection presents more than 8,800 historical maps of North and South America. Rumsey is gradually making his personal collection — previously seen by only a few hundred visitors — accessible in two formats: a standard browser designed for the general public and one requiring Insight software (available for free download) for more serious researchers. Most of the maps were made in the eighteenth and nineteenth centuries; many are notable for their craftsmanship. Materials include atlases, globes, books, maritime charts, pocket and wall maps, and children's maps. Users can zoom in to view details. Overlay capabilities make this website valuable for its ability to convey ways that locations have changed over time.

### 113. Dime Novels and Penny Dreadfuls
*Stanford University*
http://www-sul.stanford.edu/depts/dp/pennies

This website presents 2,364 images of covers as well as nine full-text selections of American "dime novels" and their British counterparts, the "penny dreadfuls." Materials also include weekly story papers that flourished in the nineteenth century. The website offers "guided tours" with images and essays of approximately 1,500 words on print processes and dime novel covers. The full-text selections include stories featuring such heroes as Nick Carter, Buffalo Bill, Jesse James, Deadwood Dick, Fred Fearnot, and Calamity Jane. The website provides basic information on each title and indexes selections according to subject, genre, setting, intended audience age and gender, and type of graphic material. Subject indexing of cover iconography is especially valuable because listings are organized according to depictions of ethnicity/nationality, occupation, types of places, types of sports and recreations, types of violence, types of gestures, and actions classified according to the gender of the character portrayed.

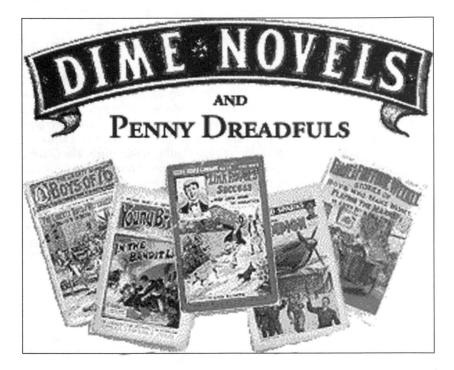

Screenshot from *Dime Novels and Penny Dreadfuls* [113].
*(Stanford University Libraries)*

**114. Disability History Museum**
*Disability History Museum*
http://www.disabilitymuseum.org/lib

This ongoing project was designed "to promote understanding about the historical experience of people with disabilities by recovering, chronicling, and interpreting their stories." The website currently presents more than 600 documents and more than 850 stills dating from the eighteenth century to the present. Subjects are organized according to categories of advocacy, types of disability, government, institutions, medicine, organizations, private life, public life, and personal names. Documents include articles, poems, pamphlets, speeches, letters, book excerpts, and editorials. Of special interest are documents from the Roosevelt Warm Springs Institute for Rehabilitation Archives, including the *Polio Chronicle*, a journal published by patients at Warm Springs, Georgia, from 1931 to 1934. Images include photographs, paintings, postcards, lithographs, children's book illustrations, and nineteenth-century family photographs, as well as postcard views of institutions, beggars, charity events, and types of wheelchairs.

## 115. Documenting the American South
*University of North Carolina, Chapel Hill, Libraries*
http://docsouth.unc.edu

Nearly 1,400 documents address aspects of life in the South from the eighteenth, nineteenth, and early twentieth centuries. The database features seven major projects. *First-Person Narratives of the American South, 1860–1920* offers 140 diaries, autobiographies, memoirs, travel accounts, and ex-slave narratives. *North American Slave Narratives, Beginnings to 1920* [81] furnishes about 250 texts. The *Library of Southern Literature* makes available fifty-one titles in southern literature. *The Church in the Southern Black Community, Beginnings to 1920* traces "how Southern African Americans experienced and transformed Protestant Christianity into the central institution of community life." *The Southern Homefront, 1861–1865* documents nonmilitary aspects of southern life. The *North Carolina Experience, Beginnings to 1940* provides approximately 575 histories, descriptive accounts, institutional reports, works of fiction, images, oral histories, and songs. *North Carolinians and the Great War* offers approximately 170 documents on effects of World War I and its legacy. All projects are accompanied by essays from the *Encyclopedia of Southern Culture*.

Screenshot from *Documenting the American South* [115].
*(Documenting the American South, The University of North Carolina at Chapel Hill Libraries)*

## 116. Evolution of the Conservation Movement, 1850–1920

*Library of Congress, American Memory*
http://lcweb2.loc.gov/ammem/amrvhtml/conshome.html

This website documents published works, manuscripts, images, and motion picture footage about the formation of the movement to conserve and protect America's natural heritage. Materials include sixty books and pamphlets, 140 federal statutes and congressional resolutions, thirty-four additional legislative documents, excerpts

Photograph from *Evolution of the Conservation Movement, 1850–1920* [116]. *(Library of Congress)*

from the *Congressional Globe* and the *Congressional Record*, 360 presidential proclamations, 170 prints and photographs, two historic manuscripts, and two motion pictures. Website visitors can view such holdings as twenty Alfred Bierstadt paintings, period travel literature, a photographic record of Yosemite, and congressional acts regarding conservation and the establishment of national parks. The website provides an annotated chronology of selected events in the development of the conservation movement with links to pertinent documents and images. Materials are searchable by subject, author, and keyword and are ideal for researching the history of national parks, nature, and conservation movements in the United States.

## 117. Great Chicago Fire and the Web of Memory

*Chicago Historical Society and Northwestern University*
http://www.chicagohs.org/fire

This exhibit commemorates the 125th anniversary of the Great Chicago Fire (1871) with an array of primary sources arranged into two sections. *The Great Chicago Fire* examines the fire through five chronological chapters, while a second section, *The Web of Memory*, focuses on the ways in which the fire has been remembered. This section presents the story through eyewitness accounts, popular illustrations, journal articles, fiction, poetry, and paintings. It also examines the legend of Mrs. O'Leary. The website furnishes galleries of images and artifacts, primary texts, songs, a newsreel, an "Interactive Panorama of Chicago, 1858," and background essays that explore the social and cultural context of the fire and its aftermath. Carl Smith, Professor of English and American Studies at Northwestern, curated the exhibit and wrote its text.

## 118. *HarpWeek*

*HarpWeek, LLC*
http://app.harpweek.com    $$

This subscription-based website presents full-text images and transcriptions from *Harper's Weekly*, beginning with its first issue in January 3, 1857, and running through 1912. At its peak, the magazine had a circulation of 300,000. *Harper's Weekly*, known as a "reform-minded journal," covered national and international events and issues during the Civil War, Reconstruction, and Gilded Age. Influential for its editorials and news stories, the magazine was also enjoyed for its fiction, biographies, sports stories, and cartoons — including scathing images of politicians by satirist Thomas Nast. Keyword searching is provided in addition to a manually created thesaurus-based index. The website includes categories by occupation type or role in society, geography, and seventy-four topics. Page images can be viewed in four sizes. These materials are valuable for studying nineteenth-century political, social, cultural, and military history. Free access to a collection of thirteen exhibits on a variety of historical topics is also provided [95].

### 119. History of the American West, 1860–1920
*Library of Congress, American Memory; Denver Public Library*
http://memory.loc.gov/ammem/award97/codhtml/hawphome.html

This website features more than 30,000 photographs taken between 1860 and 1920 of Colorado towns, landscapes, mining scenes, and members of more than forty American Indian tribes living west of the Mississippi River. Approximately 4,000 images deal with the mining industry, including labor strikes; 3,500 photographs depict Indian communities. Special presentations include a gallery of more than thirty photographs depicting the dwellings, children, and daily lives of American Indian women and more than thirty images of buildings, statues, and parks in Denver built in conformance with the turn-of-the-century "City Beautiful" movement. In addition, roughly twenty World War II–era photographs document the Tenth Mountain Division, ski troops based in Colorado who fought in Italy. Each image in these special exhibits is accompanied by a brief description. This website is keyword searchable, can be browsed by subject and title, and includes biographies of three western photographers.

### 120. Images of African Americans from the Nineteenth Century
*Schomburg Center for Research in Black Culture, New York Public Library*
http://digital.nypl.org/schomburg/images_aa19

These 500 images depict the social, political, and cultural worlds of their nineteenth-century African American subjects. Materials include prints, original negatives, and transparencies drawn from collections of family photographs, African American school photographs, and personal collections. The website can be searched through seventeen subject categories, such as family, labor, Civil War, slavery, social life and customs, and portraits. Visitors will find a list of images with brief descriptions under each subject category and a keyword search. Images download quickly and are of good quality.

### 121. Indian Peoples of the Northern Great Plains
*Montana State University*
http://libmuse.msu.montana.edu/epubs/nadb

These 685 items represent twenty-seven current and former American Indian tribes of the Northern Great Plains from 1870 to 1954. Most of the materials are photo-

Photograph from *History of the American West, 1860–1920* [119].
*(Library of Congress)*

graphs with identifying text. The collection also includes stereographs, ledger drawings, and other sketches. Users can view three unique collections. The *Barstow
Ledger Drawing Collection* offers sixty-six Crow and Gros Ventre drawings from the
late nineteenth century. A portfolio entitled *Blackfeet Indian Tipis, Design and
Legend* includes twenty-six works and an introductory essay. Another collection
offers treaties with the Assiniboine, Blackfeet, and North Piegan tribes from 1874
and 1875. Searching is available by subject, date, location, name, tribe, collection,
and artist or photographer. This valuable website documents folkways, material culture, and the history of American Indians from the Northern Great Plains region.

### 122. Kate and Sue McBeth, Missionary Teachers to the Nez Perce Indians
*University of Idaho*
http://www.lib.uidaho.edu/mcbeth

This website presents full-text letters and diaries on the lives and careers of Kate and
Sue McBeth, missionaries and teachers among the Nez Perce Indians during the
last quarter of the nineteenth century. Government documents and images pertaining to the tribe's history accompany these materials. Sue McBeth established a suc-
cessful theological seminary for Nez Perce men, collected and organized a Nez
Perce/English dictionary, and wrote journal articles. Kate McBeth provided literacy
education for Nez Perce women, taught Euro-American domestic skills, and

directed a Sabbath school and mission society. Materials include more than 150 letters, a diary, a journal, five treaties, more than seventy commission and agency reports and legislative actions, excerpts from a history of the Nez Perce, and nineteen biographies. Six maps and approximately 100 images, including thirteen illustrations depicting the 1855 Walla Walla Treaty negotiations, are also available.

### 123. Like a Family: The Making of a Southern Cotton Mill World
*University of North Carolina, Chapel Hill*
http://www.ibiblio.org/sohp/laf

A companion to the book of the same name, this website offers selected oral history resources that examine lives in southern textile mill towns from the 1880s to the 1930s. The website is divided into three sections. *Life on the Land* discusses agricultural roots of the rural South, changes in farm labor after the Civil War, and economic factors that caused the transition to mill work in the late nineteenth century. *Mill Village and Factory* describes work in the mills and life in the company mill towns. *Work and Protest* discusses labor protests of the 1920s, the formation of unions, and the textile strike of 1934. The website contains thirteen photographs and more than sixty audio clips drawn from oral history interviews with descendants of mill hands and others involved in the history of the southern textile industry. This website is ideal for studying rural southern life and labor history from Reconstruction through the 1930s.

### 124. Mark Twain in His Times
*Stephen Railton, University of Virginia*
http://etext.virginia.edu/railton

This engaging website is based on Mark Twain's works and life. Three sections focus on Twain's life and career, including the creation of his popular image, the marketing and promotion of his texts, and live performances. Five sections center on major works, including *Innocents Abroad, Tom Sawyer,* and *Pudd'nhead Wilson.* Each section is placed within a historical context. The website offers an extensive collection of text sources, including thirty-six published texts or lectures, sixteen letters, thirty-six texts and excerpts from other late-nineteenth-century authors, and twenty-five items from publishers. Additional materials include more than fifty newspaper and magazine articles, thirty-five obituary notices, 100 contemporary reviews, and hundreds of illustrations and photographs. A graphic essay explores the issue of racism through various American illustrations of "Jim" in *Huckleberry Finn.* This is an invaluable resource for studying American literature and its place within the nineteenth-century marketplace.

### 125. Native American Documents Project
*E. A. Schwartz, California State University at San Marcos*
http://www.csusm.edu/projects/nadp/nadp.htm

These four collections of data and documents address federal Indian policy in the late nineteenth century. The first set includes four annual reports from the 1870s of the Commissioner of Indian Affairs, along with appendices and a map. The second set, *Allotment Data,* traces the federal "reform" policy of dividing Indian lands into small tracts for individuals — a significant amount of which went to whites — from the 1870s to the 1910s. This set includes transcriptions of four acts of Congress, tables, and an essay analyzing the data. The third set includes 111 documents on the little-known Rogue River War of 1855 in Oregon, the reservations set up for Indian survivors, and the allotment of one of these reservations, the Siletz, in 1894. The fourth set provides the California section of an ethnographic compilation from 1952.

## 126. New York Public Library Picture Collection Online
*New York Public Library*
http://digital.nypl.org/mmpco

This eclectic collection offers 30,000 images from books and periodicals, as well as original photographs, prints, and postcards, mostly dating from before 1923. Covering more than 12,000 subjects, the website features images of Jamestown settlers, American Indians, American presidents, nineteenth-century New York architecture, slave life, women's costumes, streetcars and trains, and even insects and snakes. Bibliographical information accompanies each image. All items can be searched by keyword or browsed by a variety of category indexes. New York Public Library archives its online exhibitions at a separate website: **http://www2.nypl.org/home/research/calendar/oelist.cfm**. The twenty-five exhibits currently available deal with such subjects as nineteenth-century views of Manhattan's evolution, Harlem's African American community, exploration and traveling entertainment in the West, the search for utopias in the Western world, the Spanish-American War, performing arts, scientific and medical illustrations, maps, and photography by Lewis Hine and Bernice Abbott. The website also includes twenty-one video clips from oral histories with jazz greats.

Print from *New York Public Library Picture Collection Online* [126].
*(Picture Collection, The Branch Libraries, The New York Public Library Astor, Lenox and Tilden Foundations)*

### 127. Photographs of the American West, 1861–1912
*National Archives and Records Administration*
http://www.archives.gov/research_room/research_topics/
american_west/american_west.html

This website features 196 photographs that document westward migration and the development of America's western frontier. Photographs were taken or acquired by the following federal departments: Bureaus of Land Management, Indian Affairs, Public Roads, Weather, Agricultural Economics, and Reclamation as well as the Fish and Wildlife Service, the Geological Survey, boundary and claims commissions and arbitrations, the Corps of Engineers, the Forest Service, and the Signal Corps. Featured images, taken between 1861 and 1912, capture special events and everyday life on the frontier, from American Indian people and villages to military maneuvers to laborers and businessmen at work. Brief captions, the name of the photographer, and date (if available) accompany each photograph. Listings are arranged by subject and chronologically. An index lists the photographs by state.

### 128. Pioneering the Upper Midwest: Books from Michigan, Minnesota, and Wisconsin, ca. 1820–1910
*Library of Congress, American Memory*
http://memory.loc.gov/ammem/umhtml/umhome.html

This website charts the history of the Upper Midwest (Michigan, Minnesota, and Wisconsin) from the seventeenth century to the early twentieth century. These 138 volumes include first-person accounts, biographies, promotional literature, local histories, ethnographic and antiquarian texts, and colonial archival documents. Materials depict the region's land and resources, cross-cultural encounters, experiences of pioneers and missionaries, soldiers, immigrants, reformers, growth of communities, and development of local culture and society. Each work is available in full-text transcription or page images and is accompanied by a short summary. The website also offers a 2,000-word essay on the history of the Upper Midwest that covers the discovery, exploration, settlement, and development of the region from pre-contact to the early twentieth century; an 1873 regional map; links to more than forty related websites; and a bibliography of nine related works.

### 129. Prairie Settlement: Nebraska Photographs and Family Letters
*Library of Congress, American Memory; Nebraska State Historical Society*
http://memory.loc.gov/ammem/award98/nbhihtml

These two collections illuminate life on the Great Plains from 1862 to 1912. The 3,000 glass plate negatives depict everyday life in central Nebraska, with images of businesses, farms, people, churches, and fairs in four counties. Approximately 3,000 pages of letters describe the sojourn of the Uriah Oblinger family through Indiana, Nebraska, Minnesota, Kansas, and Missouri as they traveled to establish a homestead. Letters discuss such topics as land, work, neighbors, crops, religious meetings, grasshoppers, financial troubles, and Nebraska's Easter Blizzard of 1873. A 1,000-word essay describes the letter collection and the lives of the principal correspondents. Biographical notes are available for more than eighty of the people who corresponded with the Oblingers or were mentioned in the letters.

Photograph from *Prairie Settlement* [129].
*(Library of Congress)*

### 130. Small-Town America: Stereoscopic Views from the Robert Dennis Collection, 1850–1920
*Library of Congress, American Memory; New York Public Library*
http://memory.loc.gov/ammem/award97/nyplhtml/dennhome.html

This rich website provides more than 12,000 stereoscopic photographs that depict life in small towns, villages, rural areas, and — despite the title — cities throughout New York, New Jersey, and Connecticut from 1850 to 1920. Materials include pictures of buildings, street scenes, natural landscapes, agriculture, industry, transportation, homes, businesses, local celebrations, natural disasters, and people. Each grouping of photographs offers a short description of the contents as well as notes on the locations, medium, collection names, and digital identification information. The website also features an essay on the history of stereoscopic views and ten related website links. The website is searchable by keyword and can be browsed by subject and image name. These revealing illustrations of everyday life are valuable for studying the cultural history of the Mid-Atlantic region and southern New England.

Photograph from *Small-Town America* [130].
*(Library of Congress)*

### 131. Temperance and Prohibition
*K. Austin Kerr, Ohio State University*
http://prohibition.history.ohio-state.edu

Organized local and national campaigns to reduce the drinking of alcohol in the United States are documented on this website, along with efforts of those opposing Prohibition laws. Materials include dozens of contemporary images, speeches, newspaper and journal articles, advertisements, reports, statistical charts, and accounts. Specific topics include the Woman's Crusade of 1873–74, the Anti-Saloon League, the Ohio Dry Campaign of 1918, the evolution of the brewing industry, and Prohibition in the 1920s. There is material by and about temperance advocate Frances Willard (1838–1898), an annotated list of six links, and 500-word essays that guide users through the material.

### 132. Thomas A. Edison Papers
*Rutgers State University of New Jersey; National Park Service; New Jersey Historical Commission; Smithsonian Institution*
http://edison.rutgers.edu

A vast database of Thomas Edison's papers, this website includes 71,000 pages of correspondence, 12,000 pages of technical drawings, and more than 13,000 clippings about the inventor from 103 journals and newspapers. Processes for searching the website are complicated, but an extensive guide offers search strategies. Materials include 2,210 facsimiles of Edison patents from 1868 to 1931 for products such as the electric lamp and the phonograph. A collection of fourteen photographs, maps, and prints depicts Edison, his environs, and his inventions. The website offers a "Document Sampler" of twenty-four selections of general interest, an 8,000-word essay on Edison's companies, twenty-two pages about Edison and the development of the motion picture industry, and two chronologies. A bibliography directs visitors to seventy books and articles and twenty related websites.

## Emergence of Modern America, 1890–1930

### 133. African-American Experience in Ohio, 1852–1920: Selections from the Ohio Historical Society
*Library of Congress, American Memory; Ohio Historical Society*
http://memory.loc.gov/ammem/award97/ohshtml/aaeohome.html

The collection includes more than 30,000 items relating to African American life in Ohio between 1850 and 1920, including personal papers, association records, a plantation account book, ex-slave narratives, legal records, pamphlets, and speeches. More than 15,000 articles from eleven Ohio newspapers and the *African Methodist Episcopal Church Review*, perhaps the oldest African American periodical, are included. Also provided are more than 300 photographs of local community leaders, buildings, ex-slaves, and African American members of the military and police. Materials represent themes such as slavery, abolition, the Underground Railroad, African Americans in politics and government, and religion. Items include an extensive collection of correspondence by George A. Myers, an African American businessman and politician, and prominent political speeches.

### 134. African American Sheet Music, 1850–1920
*Library of Congress, American Memory; Brown University*
http://memory.loc.gov/ammem/award97/rpbhtml/aasmhome.html

This collection presents 1,305 pieces of sheet music composed by and about African Americans, from antebellum minstrel shows to early-twentieth-century African American musical comedies. Materials include works by renowned black composers and lyricists, such as James A. Bland, Will Marion Cook, Paul Laurence Dunbar, Bert Williams, George Walker, Alex Rogers, Jesse A. Shipp, Bob Cole, James Weldon Johnson, J. Rosamond Johnson, James Reese Europe, and Eubie Blake. A special presentation, "The Development of an African American Musical Theatre, 1865–1910," provides an overview that explores African American performers in mainstream entertainment. Subjects include racial depictions on covers and in lyrics; styles of music, such as ragtime, jazz, and spirituals; and topics addressed in lyrics, such as gender relations, urbanization, and wars. An eighty-title bibliography and fifteen-title discography are also available. Some material may be disturbing, but careful use of the website can offer insight into racial attitudes, popular culture, and stereotypes of African American culture.

Sheet music cover illustration from *African American Sheet Music, 1850–1920* [134]. *(Brown University Library)*

### 135. Amateur Athletic Foundation Virtual Archive
*Amateur Athletic Foundation of Los Angeles*
http://www.aafla.org/5va/over_frmst.htm

This website provides more than 37,000 documents (in PDF format) pertaining to official Olympics history as well as historic materials on other sports. Complete or partial runs of ten journals have been digitized, including the *Journal of Sports History* (1,512 articles from 1974–2000), *Olympic Review* (1901–2001), *Baseball Magazine* (1909–1918), *American Golfer* (1908–1911), *Golf Illustrated and Outdoor Man* (1914–1915), and *Outing* (1883–1899). New material is added regularly. The website also furnishes eleven oral histories of Southern California Olympic athletes; twenty-nine official Olympic Reports from 1896 to 1992; the full text of *This Great Symbol: Pierre de Coubertin and the Origins of the Modern Olympic Games* by John MacAloon; and recent studies of aspects of sports history. Keyword searching is available.

### 136. America at Work, America at Leisure: Motion Pictures from 1894–1915
*Library of Congress, American Memory*
http://memory.loc.gov/ammem/awlhtml/awlhome.html

This collection of 150 motion pictures produced between 1894 and 1915 deals with work, school, and leisure activities in the United States. The films include footage of the U.S. Post Office in 1903, cattle breeding, firefighters, ice manufacturing, logging, physical education classes, amusement parks, sporting events, and local festivals and parades. Each film is accompanied by a brief summary. A special presentation furnishes additional information on three categories: America at school, work, and leisure. Essays of roughly 1,000 words provide context and general descriptions of films in each category, offer fifteen illustrative photographs, and link to related films. A bibliography with twenty-seven titles provides suggestions for further reading on American labor, education, and leisure. The website is keyword searchable or can be browsed by title and subject.

### 137. American Leaders Speak: Recordings from World War I and the 1920 Election

*Library of Congress, American Memory*
http://memory.loc.gov/ammem/nfhtml

This website presents fifty-nine sound recordings of speeches by American leaders produced from 1918 to 1920 on the Nation's Forum record label. The speeches — by such prominent public figures as Warren G. Harding, James M. Cox, Calvin Coolidge, Franklin D. Roosevelt, Samuel Gompers, Henry Cabot Lodge, John J. Pershing, Will H. Hays, A. Mitchell Palmer, and Rabbi Stephen S. Wise — deal for the most part with issues and events related to World War I and the 1920 presidential election. Additional topics include social unrest, Americanism, bolshevism, taxes, and business practices. Speeches range from one to five minutes in length. A special presentation, "From War to Normalcy," introduces the collection with representative recordings, including Harding's famous pronouncement that Americans need "not nostrums but normalcy." This website includes photographs of speakers and of the actual recording disk labels, as well as text versions of the speeches.

### 138. American Variety Stage: Vaudeville and Popular Entertainment, 1870–1920

*Library of Congress, American Memory*
http://memory.loc.gov/ammem/vshtml/vshome.html

This collection documents the development of vaudeville and other popular entertainment forms from the 1870s to the 1920s. Materials include 334 English- and

Screenshot from *American Variety Stage* [138].
*(Library of Congress)*

Yiddish-language play scripts, 146 theater programs and playbills, sixty-one motion pictures, and ten sound recordings. The website also features 143 photos and twenty-nine memorabilia items documenting the life and career of magician Harry Houdini and an essay with links to specific items entitled "Houdini: A Biographical Chronology." Search by keyword or browse the subject and author indexes. The website is linked to the Library of Congress exhibition *Bob Hope and American Variety* (http://www.loc.gov/exhibits/bobhope), which charts the persistence of a vaudeville tradition in later entertainment forms.

### 139. Anti-Imperialism in the United States, 1898–1935

*Jim Zwick*
http://www.boondocksnet.com/ail98-35.html

This comprehensive website offers important texts on American imperialism and its opponents. Materials include 800 essays, speeches, pamphlets, political platforms, editorial cartoons, petitions, and pieces of literature, such as Mark Twain's anti-imperialist writings. The text of Rudyard Kipling's "The White Man's Burden" is available and is accompanied by fifty contemporary reactions. Items are arranged by document type and searchable by keyword.

## 140. Child Labor in America, 1908–1912: Photographs of Lewis W. Hine

*The History Place*

http://www.historyplace.com/unitedstates/childlabor

This website furnishes sixty-four photographs taken by Lewis W. Hine (1874–1940) between 1908 and 1912. Images document American children working in mills, mines, streets, and factories, and as "newsies," seafood workers, fruit pickers, and salesmen. The website also includes photographs of immigrant families and children's "pastimes and vices." Original captions by Hine — one of the most influential photographers in American history — call attention to exploitative and unhealthy conditions for laboring children. A background essay introduces Hine and the history of child labor in the United States. This is a valuable collection for studying documentary photography, urban history, labor history, and the social history of the Progressive era. *The History Place* is an advertiser-supported "private, independent, Internet-only publication based in the Boston area" that is owned and published by Philip Gavin.

Photograph from *Child Labor in America, 1908–1912* [140].
*(Lewis Hine/Courtesy of* The History Place*)*

### 141. Chinese in California, 1850–1925
*Library of Congress, American Memory; University of California,*
*Berkeley; California Historical Society*
http://lcweb2.loc.gov/ammem/award99/cubhtml/cichome.html

These 8,000 items document the immigrant experience of Chinese who settled in California during the nineteenth and early twentieth centuries. Materials include photographs, letters, diaries, speeches, business records, legal documents, pamphlets, sheet music, cartoons, and artwork. Access is provided through nine galleries, each containing an introductory essay and seventy to 575 items. Four galleries present materials on San Francisco's Chinatown, including architectural space, business and politics, community life, and appeal to outsiders. Additional galleries deal with Chinese involvement in U.S. expansion westward, communities outside San Francisco, agricultural, fishing, and related industries, the anti-Chinese movement and Chinese exclusion, and sentiment concerning the Chinese. Visitors may search by keyword, name, subject, title, and group. The website is useful for studying ethnic history, labor history, and the history of the West as well as Chinese American history.

### 142. Clash of Cultures in the 1910s and 1920s
*Matthew Davis and Pamela Pennock, Ohio State University*
http://www.history.ohio-state.edu/projects/clash

This interpretive essay of more than 10,000 words on the culture wars of the 1910s and 1920s is organized into four sections. It offers thirty documents and seventy-five images — photographs, cartoons, posters, flyers, and maps — to provide historical context and connections between seemingly unrelated phenomena. *Prohibition* includes an exhibition of photographs, political cartoons, and documents from the Ohio Dry Campaign of 1918. *Anti-Immigration and the KKK* presents a Klansman's manual, anti-immigration magazine articles, and the text of the Immigration Act of 1924. *The New Woman* contains sections on image and lifestyle, sexuality, opposition, the African American New Woman, and work, education, and reform. The *Scopes Trial* includes documents on fundamentalism and evolution and trial transcripts. The website provides twenty-eight related links and bibliographies of forty-two titles. This valuable website, created by two doctoral students at Ohio State University, emphasizes the complexity of conflicts persistent throughout twentieth-century American history.

### 143. Digital Archive Collections at the University of Hawaii
*University of Hawaii System Libraries*
http://micro100.lib3.hawaii.edu

This website provides access to important collections documenting the history of Hawaii and Micronesia from 1834 to the 1990s. *Annexation of Hawaii* contains thousands of pages of documents concerning the U.S. plan to annex Hawaii, realized in 1898. Materials include the 1,436-page *Blount Report* of 1894–95, initiated by President Grover Cleveland, on the history of relations between the United States and Hawaii and the planned annexation; congressional debates on the Hawaii Organic Act, passed in 1900 to establish a territorial government; and Hawaiian anti-annexation petitions and protest documents from 1897–98. *Hawaii War Records* presents more than 1,300 photographs documenting the impact of World War II on Hawaii and its people. The *Trust Territories of the Pacific Islands* photo archive provides 50,000 photographs on programs in education, health, and political and economic development in the 2,100 islands of Micronesia administered by the United States from 1947 to 1994. The website also includes a collection of sixteen Hawaiian-language newspapers.

### 144. Dismuke's Virtual Talking Machine
*Michael Duus*
http://www.dismuke.org

More than 225 music selections from a private collector's 78-rpm recordings produced between 1900 and the 1930s are available on this website. Music is organized according to type of recording: acoustical (pre-1925) and electrical. There are a variety of musical styles presented — ragtime, opera, jazz, classical, marching bands, and swing. Listings for selections provide information on vocalist, band, and soloist, and include short annotations. *Dismuke's Hit of the Week,* updated weekly with one to three new audio selections, offers explanatory material. The website also presents images of approximately fifteen record labels.

Photograph from *Digital Archive Collections at the University of Hawaii* [143].
*(U.S. Navy)*

### 145. Earliest Voices: A Gallery from the Vincent Voice Library

*Historical Voices and Michigan State University's MATRIX*
http://www.historicalvoices.org/earliest_voices

These nineteen audio clips offer speeches recorded by seven turn-of-the-century public figures — William Jennings Bryan, Thomas Edison, Samuel Gompers, William McKinley, William Howard Taft, and Booker T. Washington. The clips last between one and seven minutes each and most were recorded between 1900 and 1920. Subjects of the speeches include politics, reform, socialism, isolationism, trusts, the gold standard, U.S. military force, labor issues, and race relations. The website includes transcripts of the speeches as well as 150-word biographies and three photographs of each speaker. Through digitization, technicians have improved the sound quality of these recordings, some of which had become nearly inaudible. This is an opportunity to experience the oratorical powers of influential men from the early twentieth century. This site is part of *HistoricalVoices.org*, a digital library with a number of audio collections, including *Studs Terkel: Conversations with America* [202] and *Flint Sit-Down Strike* [191].

### 146. Edward S. Curtis's "The North American Indian"

*Library of Congress, American Memory; Northwestern University Library*
http://lcweb2.loc.gov/ammem/award98/ienhtml/curthome.html

This website presents all 2,226 photographs taken by Edward S. Curtis for his work *The North American Indian*. These striking images of North American tribes are considered some of the most significant representations of "the old time Indian, his dress, his ceremonies, his life and manners" ever produced. Each image is accompanied by com-

Photograph from *Edward S. Curtis's "The North American Indian"* [146].
*(Library of Congress)*

prehensive identifying data and Curtis's original captions. The voluminous collection and narrative are presented in twenty volumes, searchable by subject, eighty American Indian tribes, and seven geographic locations. This website also features a twelve-item bibliography and three scholarly essays discussing Curtis' methodology as an ethnographer, the significance of his work to Native peoples of North America, and his promotion of the twentieth-century view that American Indians were a "vanishing race." The biographical timeline and map depicting locations where Curtis photographed American Indian groups are especially useful.

### 147. Emergence of Advertising in America, 1850–1920

*John W. Hartman Center and Digital Scriptorium, Duke University*
http://scriptorium.lib.duke.edu/eaa

These 9,000 advertising items and publications date from 1850 to 1920. Selected items illustrate the rise of consumer culture in America and the development of a professionalized advertising industry. Images are grouped into eleven categories: advertising ephemera (trade cards, calendars, almanacs, postcards); broadsides for placement on walls, fences, and buildings; advertising cookbooks from food companies and appliance manufacturers; early advertising agency publications created to promote the concepts and methods of the industry; promotional literature from one of the nation's oldest advertising agencies, J. Walter Thompson Company; early Kodak print advertisements; Lever Brothers Lux (soap) advertisements; outdoor advertising; and tobacco ads. Each category contains a brief overview, and each image is accompanied by production information. The website, searchable by keyword or ad contents, includes a timeline on the history of advertising from the 1850s to 1920. This easy-to-use collection is ideal for researching consumer culture and marketing strategies.

### 148. Emma Goldman Papers

*Berkeley Digital Library*

http://sunsite.berkeley.edu/Goldman

This collection of primary resources centers on Emma Goldman (1869–1940), a major figure in the history of radicalism and feminism in the United States prior to her deportation in 1919. Materials include selections from four books by Goldman; twelve published essays and pamphlets; four speeches; forty-nine letters; five newspaper accounts of her activities; nearly forty photographs, illustrations, and facsimiles of documents; and a 1934 newsreel in which Goldman answers questions by reporters. Additional items include two biographical exhibitions, four sample documents from the book edition of her papers; and a curriculum for students to aid the study of freedom of expression, women's rights, antimilitarism, and social change. The website offers essays on the project's history and bibliographic references.

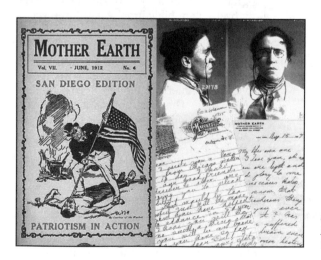

Collage from *Emma Goldman Papers* [148].
*(University of California, Berkeley)*

**149. First World War: The War to End All Wars**
*Michael Duffy*
http://www.firstworldwar.com

The stated purpose of this website is to provide an overview of World War I. This it does effectively through more than sixty essays, hundreds of encyclopedic entries, and a timeline. Primary documents include 252 resources on the war's major diplomatic and military events, eighty-three diaries and firsthand accounts of soldiers and politicians, 139 photographs, and 150 audio files of songs and speeches. Documents include treaties, reports, correspondence, memoirs, speeches, dispatches, and accounts of battles and sieges. The website also provides sixty-nine essays on literary figures who wrote about the war. While admittedly not a "professional website" and a work-in-progress, the website offers much material on the leaders who engaged their countries in war and on the experiences of ordinary soldiers who fought the battles.

**150. Florida State Archives Photographic Collection**
*Joan Morris, Florida State Archive*
http://www.floridamemory.com/PhotographicCollection

More than 100,000 photographs, many focusing on specific localities from the mid-nineteenth century to the present, are available on this website. The collection is searchable by subject, photographer, keyword, and date. Materials include collections on agriculture, the Seminole Indians, state political leaders, Jewish life, family life, postcards, and tourism. Educational units address fifteen topics, including the Civil War in Florida, educator Mary McLeod Bethune, folklorist and writer Zora Neale Hurston, pioneer feminist Roxcy Bolton, the civil rights movement in Florida, and school busing during the 1970s. An interactive timeline presents materials — including audio and video files — on Florida at war, economics and agriculture, geography and the environment, government and politics, and state culture and history.

**151. Foreign Relations of the United States, 1900–1918**
*University of Wisconsin, Madison, Libraries*
http://libtext.library.wisc.edu/FRUS

Published annually by the State Department, *Foreign Relations of the United States* (*FRUS*) is the official record of major declassified U.S. foreign policy decisions and diplomatic activity. Documents included have been selected for their ability to illuminate "policy formulation and major aspects and repercussions of its execution." *FRUS* publishes some documents years after their issuance, so there is no material on World War I or the Russian Revolution. Each volume contains an annual message from the U.S. president, circulars, and chapters devoted to individual nations. Documents pertain to a wide range of topics and are indexed at the back of each volume. Visitors may search volumes individually or the whole set by keyword, subject, and date. The website is valuable for researching diplomatic history of the early twentieth century. *FRUS* volumes for 1945 to 1972 are available separately [211].

### 152. Great American Speeches: Eighty Years of Political Oratory
*Public Broadcasting System (PBS)*
http://www.pbs.org/greatspeeches

Produced as a companion website to a PBS miniseries, this collection presents roughly 150 texts of speeches delivered between 1900 and the present. Speakers include several presidents, such as Franklin Delano Roosevelt and Calvin Coolidge; historian and African American activist W. E. B. Du Bois; anarchist Emma Goldman; suffragist Anna Howard Shaw; and politician William Jennings Bryan. Many speeches are accompanied by explanations, and some audio and brief video excerpts are included. The speeches are arranged chronologically and grouped into decades from 1900 to 1990 with accompanying timelines of historical events. The website also offers links to interactive websites on historical trivia, vocabulary, and analysis pertaining to the speeches.

### 153. Harlem: Mecca of the New Negro
*Electronic Text Center, University of Virginia*
http://etext.lib.virginia.edu/harlem

This website presents the complete facsimile and transcript versions of the March 1925 *Survey Graphic* special "Harlem Number," edited by Alain Locke. Locke later republished and expanded the contents as the famous *New Negro* anthology. The effort constituted "the first of several attempts to formulate a political and cultural representation of the New Negro and the Harlem community" of the 1920s. The journal is divided into three sections: "The Greatest Negro Community in the World," "The Negro Expresses Himself," and "Black and White — Studies in Race Contacts." The website also includes essays by Locke, W. E. B. Du Bois, and James Weldon Johnson; poems by Countee Cullen, Anne Spencer, Angelina Grimké, Claude McKay, Jean Toomer, and Langston Hughes; and quotations from reviews of the issue.

### 154. Inventing Entertainment: The Early Motion Pictures and Sound Recordings of the Edison Companies
*Library of Congress, American Memory*
http://lcweb2.loc.gov/ammem/edhtml/edhome.html

This excellent website features 341 early motion pictures from 1891 to 1896, eighty-one sound recordings from 1913 to 1920, and related materials, such as photographs and original magazine articles documenting Thomas Edison's impact on the history of American entertainment. Edison's inventions included the phonograph, the kinetograph motion picture camera, and the kinetoscope motion picture viewer. Sound recordings are accessible by title and according to six genres: instrumental selections, popular vocals, spoken word, spoken comedy, foreign language and ethnic recordings, and opera and concert recordings. Films are organized by title, chronologically, and according to genres, including actualities (nonfiction films), advertising, animation, drama and adventure, experimental, humorous, trick, and reenactments. Actuality subjects include disasters, expositions, famous people, foreign places, the navy, police, and fire departments, railroads, scenic America, sports and leisure, the variety stage, and war. Special pages focus on the life of the inventor and his contribution to motion picture and sound recording technologies.

### 155. Jack London's Writings

*Berkeley Digital Library SunSITE*

http://sunsite.berkeley.edu/London/Writings

The full-text versions of more than forty works by Jack London (1876–1916), a prominent early-twentieth-century writer who was also involved in the socialist movement, are available here. Materials include famous fiction, such as *The Call of the Wild* (1903), and lesser-known works, such as *War of the Classes* (1905), a collection of speeches London delivered on behalf of socialism. The website includes fifteen novels, nineteen short story collections, two collections of essays, one play, five additional published nonfiction works, and four newspaper and magazine pieces. The website is keyword searchable. There is no biographical or historical information about London and his times, but used with contextual materials, the website can be valuable for studying early-twentieth-century American literature and journalism and its relation to radical political and social currents of the time.

### 156. Jewish Women's Archive

*Gail Twersky Reimer*

http://www.jwa.org

These two exhibits and a multitude of resources are valuable for studying American Jewish women's contributions to their communities and the wider world. *Women of Valor* focuses on sixteen notable historic women — including Congresswoman Bella Abzug, radical Emma Goldman, philanthropist Rebecca Gratz, poet Emma Lazarus, actress Molly Picon, Hadassah founder Henrietta Szold, and nurse, settlement worker, and political leader Lillian Wald. Each biography furnishes more than fifty images and an essay in approximately twenty sections. *Women Who Dared* offers oral history interviews of Jewish women activists in text, audio, and video formats. This section includes seventy-three photographs, thirty-one audio clips, and transcribed text in which women comment on activism in the context of Jewish and gender identity, values, and situations and elucidate the path to activism, challenges, rewards, and impact.

### 157. Lower Manhattan Project: Observations of Life on the Lower East Side at the Turn of the Century

*William Crozier, Clarke Chambers, Patrick Costello, Chad Gaffield, Beverly Stadium*

http://acad.smumn.edu/History/contents.html

This website presents nineteen firsthand observations of everyday life in Lower Manhattan from the 1880s to the 1920s. Designed to supplement a college course, the materials include articles from popular magazines, government reports, and an exhibit on tenements. Featured authors include reformers such as Lillian Brandt, Jacob Riis, and William Dean Howells writing empathically about housing, immigration, poverty, work, and other features of urban life. A 300-word essay introduces the materials that are especially useful for studying urban history.

## 158. Marcus Garvey and Universal Negro Improvement Association Papers Project

*James S. Coleman African Studies Center, University of California at Los Angeles*

http://www.isop.ucla.edu/mgpp

Photograph from *Marcus Garvey and Universal Negro Improvement Association Papers Project* [158].
*(University of California, Los Angeles)*

The life and work of black activist Marcus Garvey (1887–1940) are presented on this website. Garvey was the leader of the Universal Negro Improvement Association (UNIA) and a strong supporter of the "back-to-Africa movement." Materials include forty documents, such as correspondence, editorials, reports of U.S. Department of Justice investigations, articles from African American newspapers, and a chapter from Garvey's autobiography. Primary documents are accompanied by fifteen background essays. The website also provides four audio clips from recordings of speeches Garvey made in 1921 and twenty-two images, including photos of Garvey, his wife, and colleagues, and facsimiles of UNIA documents.

## 159. Margaret Sanger Papers Project

*Department of History, New York University*

http://www.nyu.edu/projects/sanger

Selected materials by and about birth control pioneer Margaret Sanger (1879–1966) are provided here. A link to a companion website offers approximately 150 documents dealing with *The Woman Rebel*, Sanger's 1914 "radical feminist monthly," for which she was indicted and tried for violation of federal obscenity laws. The project plans to digitize more than 600 of Sanger's speeches and articles. Offered at present are eight transcribed items from 1911 to 1921; a letter written by Sanger in 1915; and more than fifty articles from the *Margaret Sanger Papers Project Newsletter*, some of which contain primary source materials. Materials also include eleven links to websites offering Sanger writings, a biographical essay, and a bibliography.

## 160. Medicine and Madison Avenue

*Ellen Gartrell, National Humanities Center; Digital Scriptorium, Duke University*

http://odyssey.lib.duke.edu/mma

This exhibit is designed to help users better understand the evolution and complexity of health-related marketing in the twentieth century. It provides more than 600 health-related advertisements printed in newspapers and magazines from 1910 to 1960, in addition to thirty-five supplementary documents. Ads have been organized into six categories: *Household Products; Over-the-Counter Drugs; Personal and Oral Hygiene; Vitamins, Tonics, Food, Nutrition, and Diet Aids; Institutional and Pharmaceutical;* and *Cigarettes.* Supplementary documents include internal reports from marketing companies, American Medical Association reports and editorials, Federal Trade Commission archival records, transcripts of 1930s radio commercials, and medical journal articles. Also provided is an eighty-item bibliography. The project highlights materials for case studies on Fleischmann's Yeast, Listerine, and Scott Tissue.

## 161. Museum of the City of San Francisco

*Gladys Hanson, Curator*

http://www.sfmuseum.org

These eleven exhibits address the history of California and San Francisco. Topics include the gold rush of 1849; earthquakes of 1906 and 1989; the history of the city's fire department; construction of the Golden Gate and Bay bridges; and internment of Japanese Americans during World War II. These exhibits provide timelines and links to more than 200 primary documents and images, including newspaper articles, diary entries, oral histories, photographs, political cartoons, and engravings. Two exhibits are hyperlinked chronologies pertaining to San Francisco during World War II and the rock music scene in the city from 1965 to 1969. Documents can be accessed according to subject, with more than twenty-five documents listed on the Chinese American community, fairs and expositions, and labor issues. The website also contains more than 150 biographies of prominent San Franciscans.

Photograph of the building of the Golden Gate Bridge from *Museum of the City of San Francisco* [161].
*(Courtesy of sfmuseum.org)*

## 162. Performing Arts in America, 1875–1923
*New York Public Library for the Performing Arts*
http://digital.nypl.org/lpa/nypl/sitemap/sitemap.cfm

A selection of more than 16,000 items relating to the performing arts of the late nineteenth and early twentieth centuries is offered on this website. Materials include documents, photographs, clippings, films, theater programs, and sheet music. Diverse types of material on specific performers—such as Ruth St. Denis, Loie Fuller, and Isadora Duncan—have been selected to allow focused study. More than 1,400 entries are available for photographs (entries often contain multiple images) as well as twenty-one large format clippings scrapbooks, each with more than 100 pages. The website also presents sixteen full-text books and video clips from nine early motion pictures, including a nine-minute clip featuring renowned dancer Anna Pavlova in Lois Weber's *The Dumb Girl of Portici* (1914). Keyword searching is available, and items can be browsed by format, name, title, and subject.

## 163. Photographs from the *Chicago Daily News:* 1902–1933
*Library of Congress, American Memory; Chicago Historical Society*
http://memory.loc.gov/ammem/ndlpcoop/ichihtml/cdnhome.html

More than 55,000 photographs taken by staff photographers of the *Chicago Daily News* during the first decades of the twentieth century are available on this website. Roughly 20 percent of the photos were published in the paper. Costing one cent for many years, the *Chicago Daily News* was an afternoon paper with stories that tried to appeal to the city's large working-class audience. The website provides subject access to the photographs, including street scenes, buildings, prominent people, labor violence, political campaigns and conventions, criminals, ethnic groups, workers, children, actors, and disasters. Many photographs of athletes and political leaders are also featured. Most of the images were taken in Chicago and nearby areas, but some were taken elsewhere, including presidential inaugurations. The images provide a glimpse into varied aspects of urban life and document the use of photography by the press during the early twentieth century.

## 164. Reclaiming the Everglades: South Florida's Natural History, 1884–1934
*Library of Congress, American Memory; University of Miami; Florida International University; Historical Museum of Southern Florida*
http://memory.loc.gov/ammem/award98/fmuhtml

This archive contains primary and secondary sources relating to reclamation efforts in the Everglades and the history of south Florida from 1884 to 1934. Comprising nearly 10,000 pages and images, the compilation includes personal correspondence; government publications, reports, and memos; and images, such as photographs, maps, and postcards. Materials document issues relating to the creation of national parks, including conflicting interests—public, private individual, and corporate—and government accountability. The website also presents a photo exhibit called *The Everglades: Exploitation and Conservation,* accompanied by a 1,000-word essay. Two additional features, an interactive timeline and thirty-one biographies of south Florida's most notable personalities, complete this project. This website is of interest for those exploring the establishment of the Everglades National Park, the con-

Historical map from *Reclaiming the Everglades: South Florida's Natural History, 1884–1934* [164]. *(Historical Museum of Southern Florida)*

servation movement, and the treatment of American Indians, particularly the Seminoles.

### 165. Red Hot Jazz Archive: A History of Jazz before 1930
*Scott Alexander*
http://www.redhotjazz.com

This comprehensive website offers biographical information, photographs, and audio and video files for more than 200 jazz bands and musicians active from 1895 to 1929. It includes more than 200 sound files of jazz recordings by well-known artists, such as Louis Armstrong, Sidney Bechet, and Django Reinhardt, and by dozens of lesser-known musicians. The files are annotated with biographical essays of varying length, discographies, and bibliographic listings. Listings are available for twenty short jazz films made in the late 1920s and early 1930s as well as two video files. Twenty essays and articles about jazz before 1930 come from published liner notes, books, journals, or jazz fans.

### 166. Sentenaryo/Centennial: The Philippine Revolution and the Philippine-American War
*Jim Zwick*
http://www.boondocksnet.com/centennia

This extensive resource explores the history of U.S. imperialism and its impact on both U.S. and Philippine history and culture. Topics include *The United States on the Eve of Empire,* the *Spanish-American War, Images of War and Empire,* and *Nation, Race, and Gender.* This website offers more than 2,000 pages and more than 750 graphics, including many of Mark Twain's anti-imperialist writings, primary documents — ranging from contemporary articles to literature and songs — and hundreds of scholarly essays. Flashing advertisements are the main disadvantage.

## 167. SIRIS Image Gallery: Selections from Archives Center

*National Museum of American History, Smithsonian Institution*

**http://sirismm.si.edu/siris/acahtop.htm**

This site presents four collections of nearly 30,000 images from the Smithsonian's vast holdings, with a link to more than 90,000 additional images in the Institution's other archives. All enlarge to high-quality images. The *Underwood and Underwood Glass Stereograph Collection, 1895–1921* of 27,622 photographs is indexed according to countries and states, interesting people, and 156 subject categories, including actors, African Americans, disasters, ethnic humor, immigration, Indians, labor, presidents, women, and World War I. A collection of thirty-two photographs by Addison N. Scurlock presents images from African American universities. Also provided are a collection of 1,591 soap advertisements from 1889 to 1998, mostly in the *Ivory Soap Advertising Collection*, and a postcard collection of 169 images from 1880 to 1975. Users may go to the *Full Archives Catalog* and search for additional digitized images by clicking on "Combined" then inputting "jpg" and appropriate search terms. This is not the easiest site to use, but the amount of material available makes it valuable to those studying aspects of American history.

## 168. South Texas Border, 1900–1920: Photographs from the Robert Runyon Collection

*Library of Congress, American Memory; University of Texas, Austin*

**http://memory.loc.gov/ammem/award97/txuhtml/runyhome.html**

Photograph from *South Texas Border, 1900–1920* [168].
*(Robert Runyon Photograph Collection, Center for American History, Ut-Austin, E/VN 08775)*

This collection featuring the work of commercial photographer Robert Runyon (1881–1968) totals more than 8,000 images that document the history and development of south Texas and the border. Topics include the U.S. military presence in the area prior to and during World War I and the growth and development of the Rio Grande Valley in the early 1900s. A special section presents nine of Runyon's 350 photographs of the Mexican Revolution (1910–1920) in Matamoros, Monterrey, Ciudad Victoria, and the Texas border area from 1913 through 1916. The website also offers essays on the revolution and on Runyon.

## 169. The Spanish-American War in Motion Pictures

*Library of Congress, American Memory*

**http://memory.loc.gov/ammem/sawhtml/sawhome.html**

This website features sixty-eight motion pictures from the Spanish-American War and the Philippine Revolution produced by the Edison Manufacturing Company and the American Mutoscope and Biograph Company between 1898 and 1901. These films include footage of troops, ships, notable figures, and parades shot in the United States, Cuba, and the Philippines, in addition to reenactments of battles and related events. *Special Presentation* puts the motion pictures in chronological order, and brief essays provide a historical context for the filming. This website is indexed by subject, is searchable by keyword, and includes a link to resources and documents pertaining to the war in the Library of Congress's Hispanic Division. This website is important not only for its subject matter but because it shows how people from this period experienced war.

### 170. Stars and Stripes: The American Soldiers' Newspaper of World War I, 1918–1919

*Library of Congress, American Memory*

http://memory.loc.gov/ammem/sgphtml/sashtml

This collection presents the complete run — from February 8, 1918, to June 13, 1919 — of the "official newspaper" of U.S. Army fighting forces. The American Expeditionary Forces (AEF) were formed in May 1917 following U.S. entrance into World War I. *Stars and Stripes* was created by order of the AEF supreme commander, General John J. Pershing, to strengthen morale and promote unity among soldiers. Professionals from the newspaper industry joined the staff, including a few well-known journalists. At its peak, the weekly newspaper reached more than a half million soldiers, providing news of the war, sports reports, cartoons, news from home, and poetry. A special presentation discusses the newspaper's contents, staff, advertising, military censorship, the AEF, and the role women played in the war effort. Search the full text or browse individual issues.

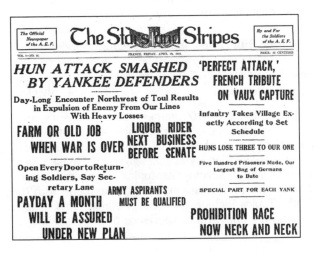

Screenshot from *Stars and Stripes: The American Soldiers' Newspaper of World War I, 1918–1919* [170].
*(Library of Congress)*

### 171. Touring Turn-of-the-Century America: Photographs from the Detroit Publishing Company, 1880–1920

*Library of Congress, American Memory*

http://memory.loc.gov/ammem/detroit/dethome.html

The Detroit Publishing Company mass-produced photographic images — especially color postcards, prints, and albums — for the American market from the late 1890s to 1924. This collection of more than 25,000 glass negatives and transparencies and about 300 color photolithographs also includes images taken prior to the company's formation by landscape photographer William Henry Jackson, who became the company's president in 1898. Jackson's work documenting western sites influenced the conservation movement. Although many images were taken in eastern locations, other areas of the United States, the Americas, and Europe are represented. The collection specializes in views of buildings, streets, colleges, universities, natural landmarks, resorts, and copies of paintings. More than 300 photographs were taken in Cuba during the Spanish-American War. About 900 mammoth plate photographs include views of Hopi peoples and their crafts and landscapes along several railroad lines in the 1880s and 1890s.

### 172. Traveling Culture: Circuit Chautauqua in the Twentieth Century

*Library of Congress, American Memory; University of Iowa Libraries*

http://memory.loc.gov/ammem/award98/iauhtml

This website provides access to roughly 8,000 publicity brochures, advertisements, and circulars from a booking agency that represented 4,546 lecturers and performers appearing on the midwest Chautauqua circuit mostly between 1890 and 1940. Talent traveled the circuit to perform during the summer in a large tent set up each week in a different town. An eclectic variety of acts participated, including international cookery experts, Helen Keller, jiujitsu masters, William Jennings Bryan, documentary filmmakers, and yodeling troupes. An essay introduces the Chautauqua phenomenon. Materials are searchable by subject, keyword, or name. The website also contains links to four other websites about Chautauqua and four websites about the history of American entertainment. This website is a delightful resource for studying popular culture, entertainment, and advertising.

### 173. Urban Experience in Chicago: Hull-House and Its Neighborhoods, 1889–1963

*University of Illinois at Chicago; Jane Addams Hull-House Museum*

http://www.uic.edu/jaddams/hull/urbanexp

This well-organized website offers more than 700 items — including newspaper, magazine, and journal articles, letters, memoirs, reports, maps, and photographs. Materials are embedded within a clear historical narrative that illuminates the life of Jane Addams in addition to the history and legacy of Chicago's Hull House. Users can search the website or focus on any of seventy-five topics arranged in eleven chapters that begin with settlement life in Chicago in the 1880s and end with the movement after Addams's death. Topics include the reform climate in Chicago, activism within the movement, and the immigrant experience of race, citizenship, and community. Additional materials address education within the settlement house and cultural and leisure activities at Hull House and in Chicago. The website provides a timeline featuring a pictorial biography of Addams and a geographical section that includes nationality maps of Chicago.

### 174. USC Archival Research Center
*University of Southern California, Information Services*
http://www.usc.edu/isd/archives/arc

These varied collections of materials document Los Angeles history. *Digital Archives* offers more than 8,000 photographs, maps, manuscripts, texts, and sound recordings in addition to exhibits. Nearly 1,200 images of artifacts from early Chinese American settlements in Los Angeles and Santa Barbara are available, as is the entire run of *El Clamor Publico*, considered the city's main Spanish-language newspaper from the 1850s. Photographs document Japanese American relocation during World War II, and photographs, documents, and oral history audio files record Korean American history. The archive also includes Works Projects Administration Land Use survey maps and Auto Club materials. Website exhibits emphasize the city's architectural history. A related exhibit, *Los Angeles: Past, Present, and Future* (http://www.usc.edu/isd/archives/la), offers collections on additional topics, including discovery and settlement, California missions, electric power, "murders, crimes, and scandals," city neighborhoods, cemeteries, Disneyland, African American gangs, and the Red Car lines.

### 175. U.S. Steel Gary Works Photograph Collection, 1906–1971
*Indiana University Northwest; Calumet Regional Archives*
http://www.dlib.indiana.edu/collections/steel

This website presents more than 2,200 images of the Gary Works Steel Mill and the corporate town of Gary, Indiana. A tour introduces thirty-six photographs with inter-

Photograph from *U.S. Steel Gary Works Photograph Collection, 1906–1971* [175]. *(Calumet Regional Archives, Indiana University Northwest)*

pretive text documenting the creation of the mill, which opened in 1908, and life in Gary among the workers, a varied group of immigrants representing fifty-two nationalities. Search by keyword or browse by subject and date to learn about this planned industrial community. Subject headings include the steel mill and its workers; factories and furnaces; houses and office buildings; women, children, and welfare facilities; and accidents. *Contextual Materials* presents an introductory essay, four magazine articles dating from 1907 to 1913, six book excerpts from 1911 to 1986, a bibliography of nearly eighty items, and links to additional information about Gary and steelmaking.

### 176. Votes for Women: Selections from the National American Woman Suffrage Association Collection, 1848–1921

*Library of Congress, American Memory*

**http://memory.loc.gov/ammem/naw/nawshome.html**

This collection includes 167 books, pamphlets, handbooks, reports, speeches, and other artifacts, totaling some 10,000 pages, dealing with the suffrage movement in America. Formed in 1890 from two rival groups, the National American Woman Suffrage Association (NAWSA) orchestrated passage of the Nineteenth Amendment in 1920 through state campaigns. Materials include works by Carrie Chapman Catt, the Association's longtime president, as well as those from other officers and members, including Elizabeth Cady Stanton, Susan B. Anthony, Lucy Stone, Alice Stone Blackwell, Julia Ward Howe, Elizabeth Smith Miller, and Mary A. Livermore. There are two bibliographies, an essay on Catt, a timeline, and links to eleven related collections. A related website, *By Popular Demand: "Votes for Women" Suffrage Pictures, 1850–1920* (**http://memory.loc.gov/ammem/vfwhtml/vfwhome.html**) is also valuable.

### 177. Wisconsin Historical Images

*Wisconsin Historical Society Digital Library and Archives*

**http://www.wisconsinhistory.org/whi**

These several thousand photographs — as well as a few posters and paintings, advertising material, ephemera, and political cartoons — present images of people and places in Wisconsin from 1870 to 1970. Materials are accessible by broad categories — such as agriculture, disasters, domestic life, education, ethnic groups, health, Indians, organizations, political activities, recreation, rural, urban, women, and work. Or search by image title, description, creator, location, or subject term.

Cartoon at *Votes for Women: Selections from the National American Woman Suffrage Association Collection, 1848–1921* [176].
*(Library of Congress)*

**178. Without Sanctuary: Photographs and Postcards of Lynching in America**

*James Allen and Journal E (Musarium)*

http://www.musarium.com:16080/withoutsanctuary

This collection, assembled by James Allen, presents chilling images taken at lynchings throughout America, primarily from the late nineteenth and early twentieth centuries. Many were circulated as souvenir postcards. The website is a companion to Allen's book *Without Sanctuary*. The exhibit can be experienced through a Flash movie with narrative comments by Allen or as a gallery of more than eighty photographs with brief captions. Most images also have links to more extensive descriptions of the circumstances behind each specific act of violence. Although the vast majority of lynching victims were African American, white victims are also depicted. These images are disturbing and difficult to fathom. They provide, however, an excellent resource for approaching the virulence and impact of racism in America.

**179. World War I Document Archive**

*Jane Plotke, Richard Hacken, Alan Albright, and Michael Shackelford*

http://www.lib.byu.edu/~rdh/wwi

Hundreds of documents and thousands of images relating to World War I, with particular emphasis on military, diplomatic, and political dimensions, are available on this website. Documents are arranged chronologically and by type, including more than 100 official documents from sixteen countries, 100 personal reminiscences, and twenty-four treaties from 1856 to 1928. A photo archive provides 1,844 images in fifteen categories, including individuals, locations, heads of state, commanders, refugees, and war albums. The website also offers substantial sections on the maritime war and the medical front, a biographical dictionary for 200 names; a bibliographical essay covering 100 titles; and approximately 125 links to related websites. The authors — volunteers from a World War I electronic discussion network — encourage user participation in expanding the website, a valuable source for studying military and diplomatic aspects of the war.

## Great Depression and World War II, 1929–1945

**180. Ad*Access**

*Digital Scriptorium, Duke University*

http://scriptorium.lib.duke.edu/adaccess

This well-developed website presents images of more than 7,000 advertisements printed primarily in newspapers and magazines in the United States from 1911 to 1955. The material is drawn from a collection of one of the oldest and largest advertising agencies, the J. Walter Thompson Company. Advertisements are divided into five main subject areas: *Radio* (including radios and programs); *Television* (including television sets and programs); *Transportation* (including airlines, rental cars, buses, trains, and ships); *Beauty and Hygiene* (including cosmetics, soaps, and shaving supplies); and *World War II* (U.S. government–related, such as V-mail and bond drives). Ads are searchable by keyword, type of illustration, and special features. A timeline from 1915 to 1955 provides general context. *About Ad Access* furnishes an overview of advertising history, as well as a bibliography and list of advertising repositories.

### 181. After the Day of Infamy: "Man on the Street" Interviews Following the Attack on Pearl Harbor
*Library of Congress, American Memory*
http://memory.loc.gov/ammem/afcphhtml/afcphhome.html

This collection includes more than twelve hours of audio interviews conducted in the days following the December 7, 1941, attack on Pearl Harbor and in January and February 1942. Interviews include the voices of 200 "ordinary Americans" recorded in ten places across the United States. December recordings were made by field-workers contacted by the Library of Congress Radio Research Project to gather opinions of a diverse group of citizens regarding U.S. entrance into war. In the 1942 recordings, produced by the Office of Emergency Management, interviewees were instructed to speak their minds directly to President Roosevelt. Interviewees discuss domestic issues, including racism and labor activism, in addition to the war. Related written documents and biographies of the fieldworkers are also presented. The interviews are available in audio files and text transcriptions and are searchable by keyword, subject, and location.

### 182. Albert and Vera Weisbord Archives
*Albert and Vera Weisbord Foundation*
http://www.weisbord.org

This archive contains the transcribed public papers of Albert and Vera Weisbord, American communists active from the 1920s to the 1970s. The website contains a biographical introduction and seven volumes of *Class Struggle* from 1931 to 1937, a journal the Weisbords edited and to which Albert was the main contributor. In addition, visitors may read the preface, introduction, and a review of Albert's book, *The Conquest of Power*. The bulk of the material contains transcriptions of approximately seventy-five articles by Albert and Vera on topics such as the 1926 textile strike in Passaic, New Jersey, the Spanish Revolution, big business, scientific material-ism, "Moscow's Betrayal of the Cuban Revolution," "The Struggle for Negro Emancipation," and "The Coming Dissolution of NATO." There are twenty-five articles from the 1970s journal *La Parola del Popolo*. Material is indexed by title within subject categories, but no subject search is available.

### 183. America from the Great Depression to World War II: Photographs from the FSA-OWI, 1935–1945
*Library of Congress, American Memory*
http://memory.loc.gov/ammem/fsowhome.html

This website features more than 160,000 images taken by government photographers with the Farm Security Administration (FSA) and the Office of War Information (OWI) during the New Deal and World War II. This period was marked by an impulse to capture in writing, sounds, and images significant aspects of American life and traditions. These photographs document the ravages of the Great Depression, scenes of everyday life in small towns and cities, and mobilization campaigns for World War II. This website includes approximately 1,600 color photographs and selections from two popular collections: *"Migrant Mother" Photographs* and *Photographs of Signs Enforcing Racial Discrimination.* The website also provides a bibliography, a background essay, six short biographical sketches of FSA-OWI photographers Ben Shahn, John Vachon, Dorothea Lange, Walker Evans, Arthur Rothstein, and Gordon Parks, and links to seven related websites. This is a great source for studying the documentary expression of the 1930s and 1940s.

### 184. American Life Histories: Manuscripts from the Federal Writers' Project, 1936–1940
*Library of Congress, American Memory*
http://memory.loc.gov/ammem/wpaintro/wpahome.html

This website features approximately 2,900 life histories from 1936 to 1940 written by the staff of the Folklore Project. These writers participated in the Federal Writers' Project for the U.S. Works Progress (later Work Projects) Administration (WPA). Documents represent the work of more than 300 writers from twenty-four states. The histories, usually between 2,000 and 15,000 words in length, take the form of narratives, dialogues, reports, and case histories. Drafts and revisions are included. A typical history may offer information on family life, education, income, occupation, political views, religion, mores, medical needs, diet, and observations on society and culture. *Voices from the Thirties,* illustrated with photographs of the project's staff at work, interviewees, and their environment, provides contextual information on the creation of the collection. This multifaceted website offers firsthand accounts on subjects such as slavery, nineteenth-century American folk cultures, and the social history of the Great Depression.

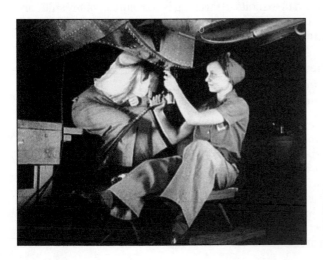

"Rosie the Riveter" photograph at *America from the Great Depression to World War II* [183].
*(Library of Congress)*

## 185. Ansel Adams's Photographs of Japanese American Internment at Manzanar
*Library of Congress, American Memory*
http://memory.loc.gov/ammem/aamhtml/aamhome.html

During World War II, the U.S. government forced more than 100,000 Japanese Americans to leave their homes and businesses, relocating them to internment camps from California to Arkansas. Well-known photographer Ansel Adams documented the lives of Japanese Americans at the Manzanar War Relocation Center in California — from portraits to daily life, including agriculture and leisure. This website presents 242 original negatives and 209 photographic prints, often displayed together to show Adams's developing and cropping techniques. His 1944 book on Manzanar, *Born Free and Equal*, is also reproduced. Adams donated the collection to the Library of Congress in 1965, writing, "The purpose of my work was to show how these people, suffering under a great injustice . . . had overcome the sense of defeat and dispair [sic] by building for themselves a vital community in an arid (but magnificent) environment."

## 186. Archives of American Art, Oral History Collections
*Smithsonian Institution, Archives of American Art*
http://www.archivesofamericanart.si.edu/collectn.htm

This collection offers hundreds of transcriptions of oral history interviews with American artists and photographers, many of whom were active in Works Projects Administration (WPA) artist projects. Interviews with WPA-employed artists were conducted as part of a 1960s oral history project. The website also provides transcripts of interviews with Federal Art Project administrators and sixteen sound excerpts of selected interviews. Non-WPA transcriptions include interviews with well-known artists from later periods. Summary information on each interview can be found by selecting the link for *SIRIS* — the Smithsonian Institution's online catalog [167] — and searching on a particular name. To separate WPA interviews from the others offered, search on *New Deal and the Arts Oral History Project*. The website also furnishes twenty-five small exhibits. Searching is not simple, but results are rewarding for studying New Deal arts projects and the work of twentieth-century American artists and photographers.

## 187. By the People, For the People: Posters from the WPA, 1936–1943
*Library of Congress, American Memory*
http://memory.loc.gov/ammem/wpaposters/wpahome.html

This colorful exhibit showcases more than 900 Work Projects Administration (WPA) silkscreen, lithograph, and woodcut posters produced from 1936 to 1943 as part of the New Deal program to support the arts during the Great Depression. Posters promoted New Deal and local programs dealing with health, safety, education, travel, and tourism, as well as publicizing art exhibits, theater and musical performances, and community activities in seventeen states and the District of Columbia. Each poster is accompanied by a brief description. Three special presentations furnish more than forty posters selected to represent the collection's breadth and depth as well as style and content; an audio recording with a silkscreen artist; and a Federal

Art Project calendar. A bibliography of ten related scholarly works also is included. The website is keyword searchable and allows browsing.

### 188. Club Kaycee, Golden Age of Kansas City Jazz
*Miller Nichols Library, University of Missouri, Kansas City*
http://www.umkc.edu/orgs/kcjazz/mainpage.htm

These forty-three audio files present Kansas City jazz recordings that span 1906 to 1954. Most were recorded during the city's "Golden Age" — from the late 1920s to the early 1940s. Short profiles are provided on twenty-eight jazz artists, including Count Basie, Charlie Parker, Lester Young, Big Joe Turner, Benny Moten, and Andy Kirk. Materials also include articles on the Eighteenth and Vine district, "internationally recognized as one of the cradles of jazz"; the Coon-Sanders Original Nighthawks Orchestra, the first Kansas City jazz band to become known nationwide in the 1920s; and Kansas City clubs and nightspots. An annotated bibliography with twenty-six titles and a discography with forty-five titles are also available. Small photographs of people and places accompany some essays. The website provides a good introduction to this important center of jazz creation and is valuable for studying twentieth-century urban and cultural history.

### 189. Densho: The Japanese American Legacy Project
*Densho*
http://www.densho.org

"Densho" means "to pass on to the next generation." In this spirit, this website offers an archive of more than 110 oral histories in 200 hours of video interviews on Japanese American incarceration during World War II. Materials include approximately 1,000 photographs and documents. Access to archive materials requires registration, a free process that takes approximately one week. Once registered, users may select materials according to twenty-nine topics, including immigration, community, religion and churches, education, race and racism, identity values, resistance, economic loss, redress and reparations, and reflections on the past. Materials available without registration include *Causes of the Incarceration*, an exploration of four prime factors — racism, failure of leadership, wartime hysteria, and economic motives — that contributed to the internment policy. The website also offers ninety-two multimedia materials providing historical context, a timeline, and a list of related sources.

### 190. FDR Cartoon Archive
*Niskayuna High School, New York*
http://www.nisk.k12.ny.us/fdr

This collection presents thousands of political cartoons concerning the presidency of Franklin D. Roosevelt. The materials are arranged into the following categories: *The Road to Pennsylvania Avenue, Waiting for the New Deal, The First One-Hundred Days, Farm Issues, Supreme Court Reform, Foreign Relations,* and the *War Years of 1942 and 1943.* Brief background essays and questions designed to prompt further inquiries are available. The site provides the texts of Roosevelt's inaugural addresses and a page of teacher resources and suggested projects.

### 191. Flint Sit-Down Strike
*Historical Voices and Michigan State University's MATRIX*
http://www.historicalvoices.org/flint

This rich, multimedia resource provides an introduction to "the greatest strike in American history." The six-week occupation of the General Motors plant at Flint, Michigan, in 1936–37 was led by the recently formed United Auto Workers. Using the new tactic of remaining in the plant rather than picketing outside, the strikers stopped production and won many demands. The website begins with a short introductory essay and a seven-item bibliography. The three main sections — organization, strike, and aftermath — provide nearly 100 audio interviews recorded between 1978 and 1984 with former strikers recalling work conditions prior to the strike, experiences during the sit-in, the hostile reaction of Flint residents, the role of the Women's Auxiliary, and conditions following the strike. Each section includes a narrative essay. In addition the website presents slideshows, an audio timeline, and a Flash-generated strike map with textual and audio links. This site is part of HistoricalVoices.org, a digital library with a number of audio collections, including *Studs Terkel: Conversations with America* [202] and *Earliest Voices: A Gallery from the Vincent Voice Library* [145].

### 192. Franklin D. Roosevelt Presidential Library and Digital Archives
*Franklin D. Roosevelt Library and Museum, Marist College*
http://www.fdrlibrary.marist.edu

This website offers more than 10,000 documents pertaining to Franklin D. Roosevelt's presidency. Documents include approximately 6,000 pieces of formerly classified correspondence, reports, and memoranda regarding such topics as the Atlantic Charter, the United Nations, the Departments of War, Treasury, and State, and the Manhattan Project to develop the atom bomb. The website also offers 1,000 documents pertaining to United States–Vatican relations during World War II, 2,000 documents concerning United States–German relations, and full texts of thirty fireside chats. An exhibit examines the "Special Relationship" between Winston Churchill and Roosevelt and the emergence of an Anglo-American alliance. A mini-multimedia showcase contains one video clip of Roosevelt walking and eleven audio clips of speeches. The website also provides information on Eleanor Roosevelt and the Great Depression, and includes more than 2,000 photographs.

### 193. Hispano Music and Culture from the Northern Rio Grande: The Juan B. Rael Collection
*Library of Congress, American Memory*
http://memory.loc.gov/ammem/rghtml/rghome.html

This website presents approximately eight hours of religious and secular music recorded in 1940 in rural northern New Mexico and southern Colorado by Juan Bautista Rael (1900–1993), a Stanford University folklorist and linguist. The 146 titles in the collection include *alabados* (religious hymns), folk dramas, wedding songs, and dance tunes. The website also provides 218 pages of documents related to the recording trip and the music, including thirty-five pieces of correspondence, recording logs, two essays by Rael published in academic journals, and one unpublished manuscript. Additional materials include four recent essays in Spanish and English on Rael; the culture, history, and society of the *Nuevo Mexicanos*; religious and secular music in the collection; and *Hispano* folk theater in the region. The website offers a keyword search and can be browsed by performer and title.

**194. Historic Government Publications from World War II: A Digital Library**
*Southern Methodist University, Central University Libraries*
http://worldwar2.smu.edu

Currently 259 U.S. government publications from World War II have been digitized for this website, an ongoing project that plans to add another 250 documents. Materials include pamphlets and books emphasizing home front issues, such as air raids, preservation, child labor, and victory farms. All materials are searchable by title, author, subject, and keyword. Browsing is also available. A companion collection of photographs, the *Melvin C. Shaffer Collection*, depicts the home front situation in Germany, North Africa, Italy, and southern France from 1943 to 1945. Shaffer was a U.S. Army medical photographer assigned to document "the medical history of the war" through major campaigns. The photographs in this website — totaling approximately 340 — are not those he took officially but ones he shot on his own to record war's impact on civilians.

**195. Museum of the City of New York: Exhibitions**
*Museum of the City of New York*
http://www.mcny.org/Exhibitions/exhibits1.htm

More than twenty exhibitions of historical New York City images are presented on this website. *Currier and Ives, Printmakers to the American People* offers seventy-eight prints — including many idealized visions — produced in the nineteenth century for newspapers and magazines and decorative lithographs aimed at a middle- and lower-income market. *Gotham Comes of Age* presents 172 photographs from a leading commercial studio that depict street life, home life, businesses, work, and the stage from 1892 to 1942. *New York before the War* provides more than 950 photographs from the New Deal's Federal Art Project (FAP). All 307 stills from renowned photographer Berenice Abbott's *Changing New York* FAP project are also furnished. *New York during the War* presents ninety-seven stills produced by the Office of War Information for exhibits abroad designed to portray the city in a positive light. Other exhibits deal with the Astor Place riot of 1849, the consolidation of the five boroughs in 1896, and the terrorist attacks on September 11, 2001.

**196. New Deal Network**
*Franklin and Eleanor Roosevelt Institute and Institute for Learning
Technologies, Teachers College, Columbia University*
http://newdeal.feri.org

This database offers more than 20,000 items relevant to the New Deal. *Document Library* contains more than 900 newspaper and journal articles, speeches, letters, reports, advertisements, and other textual materials that treat a broad array of subjects and place special emphasis on relief agencies and issues relating to labor, edu-

Photograph from *New Deal Network* [196].
*(Franklin D. Roosevelt Library)*

cation, agriculture, the Supreme Court, and African Americans. *Photo Gallery* presents more than 5,000 images. *The Magpie Sings the Depression* presents poems, articles, short stories, and graphics from a Bronx high school journal. *Dear Mrs. Roosevelt* offers letters written by young people to the first lady. *Student Activism in the 1930s* contains photographs, graphics, cartoons, memoirs, autobiographical essays, and a 20,000-word essay on campus radicalism. The website also provides speeches and articles by Henry Wallace, a photo-documentary on a small Alabama town, and materials on the Federal Theatre Project, Tennessee Valley Authority, the Civilian Conservation Corps, and the National Youth Administration.

### 197. New Deal Stage: Selections from the Federal Theatre Project, 1935–1939
*Library of Congress, American Memory*
http://memory.loc.gov/ammem/fedtp/fthome.html

More than 13,000 images relating to the Works Progress Administration's Federal Theatre Project (FTP) are available on this website. FTP was a New Deal program designed to provide work for unemployed theater professionals and reinvigorate a treasured American institution — live theater — in serious decline. The collection contains seventy-one play scripts and 168 documents from the FTP's Administration

Records. Extensive materials, including photographs, scripts, posters, and set and costume designs, have been selected from three significant productions: *Macbeth* and *The Tragic History of Dr. Faustus*, directed by Orson Welles, and Arthur Arent's *Power*, an example of the Project's innovative "Living Newspaper" series of topical plays. The website includes a lengthy background essay, as well as four illustrated articles about FTP. It is valuable for studying the history of American theater, New Deal programs, and the 1930s movement known as the "cultural front," in which groups with a progressive vision gained a conspicuous presence in American culture.

### 198. "Now What a Time": Blues, Gospel, and the Fort Valley Music Festivals, 1938–1943

*Library of Congress, American Memory*

http://memory.loc.gov/ammem/ftvhtml/ftvhome.html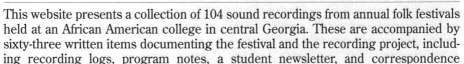

This website presents a collection of 104 sound recordings from annual folk festivals held at an African American college in central Georgia. These are accompanied by sixty-three written items documenting the festival and the recording project, including recording logs, program notes, a student newsletter, and correspondence

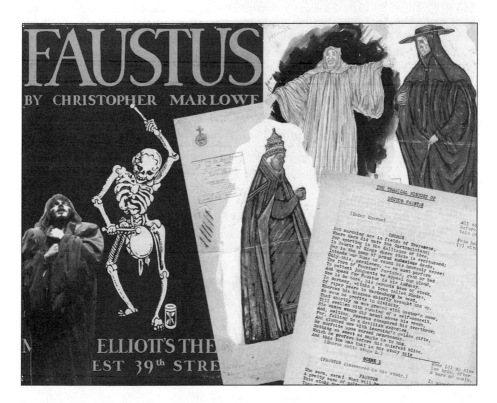

Screenshot from *New Deal Stage* [197].
*(Library of Congress)*

between the festival's cofounders and folklorists. Materials include biographies of festival founders; a *Special Presentation* entitled "Noncommercial Recordings" by Bruce Bastin, excerpted from his book *Red River Blues*; and a thirty-title bibliography. The collection is searchable by performer, title, and keyword, but lyrics are not available. The collection is a valuable record of noncommercial American music and musical styles. It is also helpful for studying broader cultural trends, such as the sixteen recordings that reflect wartime opinions and concerns.

### 199. Remembering Jim Crow
*American Radio Works*
http://www.americanradioworks.org/features/remembering

This companion website to a National Public Radio (NPR) documentary on segregation in the South presents twenty-eight audio excerpts and 130 photographs. Materials are arranged in six thematically organized sections and address legal, social, and cultural aspects of segregation, black community life, and black resistance to the Jim Crow way of life. As anthropologist Kate Ellis, one of the website's creators, notes, the interviews display a "marked contrast between African American and white reflections on Jim Crow." Many of the photographs come from personal collections of the people interviewed. The website also includes sixteen photographs taken by Farm Security Administration photographer Russell Lee in New Iberia, Louisiana. Also available are audio files and transcripts of the original radio documentary, more than seventy additional stories, a sampling of state segregation laws arranged by topic, links to eight related websites, and a bibliography with forty-one titles.

### 200. Rutgers Oral History Archives of World War II
*Sandra Stewart Holyoak, Rutgers University*
http://fas-history.rutgers.edu/oralhistory/orlhom.htm

This collection of oral history interviews centers on the home front and on men and women who served overseas during World War II. The project was started to learn more about the war from ordinary people. The archive contains 283 full-text interviews, primarily of Rutgers College and Douglass College (formerly New Jersey College for Women) alumni. Interviewers asked alumni to tell their life stories with a particular focus on the war years and postwar life under the G.I. Bill. Codes indicate the nature of interview contents and occupations of interviewees.

### 201. Southern Mosaic: The John and Ruby Lomax 1939 Southern States Recording Trip
*Library of Congress, American Memory*
http://memory.loc.gov/ammem/lohtml/lohome.html

In 1939, John Lomax, Curator of the Library of Congress Archive of American Folk Song, and his wife Ruby Terrill Lomax, embarked on a 6,500-mile journey through the South. During their travels, they recorded more than 700 folk tunes that now are available as audio files on this website. Genres include ballads, blues, children's songs, cowboy songs, field hollers, lullabies, play-party songs, spirituals, and work songs. The website also presents field notes containing personal information on some of the more than 300 performers the Lomaxes recorded, notes on geography and culture, and excerpts from correspondence. More than fifty letters to and from the Lomaxes, 381 photographs, a bibliography of twenty-three works, and a map are also offered. The website is keyword searchable and can be browsed by subject as well as title, song text, and performer.

### 202. Studs Terkel: Conversations with America

*Chicago Historical Society, Historical Voices, and Michigan State University's MATRIX*

http://www.studsterkel.org

Created to honor Studs Terkel, the noted oral historian, radio host, and Pulitzer Prize-winning author, this website makes available more than 300 audio clips of interviews Terkel conducted over fifty years. The seven galleries explore a variety of subjects, including organized labor, the 1929 stock market crash, New Deal programs, World War II, race relations, and urban life in Chicago. The interviews present well-known figures as well as lesser-heard voices, such as people traveling by train to the March on Washington in 1963. Complementing these interviews is a one-hour video interview with Terkel in which he emphasizes the importance of accurate knowledge about the past. An educational section addresses the use of oral history in the classroom. This well-designed website is valuable for studying the Great Depression, World War II, race relations, and labor issues. This site is part of *HistoricalVoices.org*, a digital library with a number of audio collections, including *Earliest Voices: A Gallery from the Vincent Voice Library* [145] and *Flint Sit-Down Strike* [191].

### 203. Voices from the Dust Bowl: The Charles L. Todd and Robert Sonkin Migrant Worker Collection, 1940–1941

*Library of Congress, American Memory*

http://memory.loc.gov/ammem/afctshtml/tshome.html

This website presents "a multi-format ethnographic field collection" that examines Depression-era migrant work camps in central California. The Farm Security

Photograph from *Voices from the Dust Bowl* [203].
*(Library of Congress)*

Administration (FSA) managed the camps, primarily inhabited by migrants from the rural areas of Oklahoma and nearby states. There are 363 audio recordings of songs, interviews, and camp announcements as well as twenty-three photographs, transcriptions of 113 songs, and a scrapbook of newspaper clippings dealing with labor and migration issues. Additional materials include eleven camp newsletters, a Works Progress Administration folk song questionnaire, field notes and correspondence of Charles L. Todd and Robert Sonkin, the original collectors of the materials, and two published magazine articles by Todd providing historical context. Topics range from camp court proceedings and personal narratives to square dances and baseball games. The website also includes a fourteen-title bibliography, a background essay, and an essay on the recording expedition. This is a valuable website for the study of Depression-era migrants, their folk traditions, and the documentary impulse of the period.

## Postwar United States, 1945 to the Early 1970s

### 204. American Radicalism Collection
*Special Collections and Digital Sources Center, Michigan State University Libraries*
http://www.lib.msu.edu/coll/main/spec_col/radicalism

This website contains images of 129 pamphlets, documents, and newsletters produced by or relevant to radical movements. Groups represented by one to thirty documents include the American Indian Movement; Asian Americans; the Black Panthers; the Hollywood Ten; the IWW; the Ku Klux Klan; the Rosenberg case; Sacco and Vanzetti; the Scottsboro Boys; and Students for a Democratic Society. Additional topics include birth control and the events at Wounded Knee. This is a small but useful website for research on radicalism, political movements, and rhetoric.

### 205. Central High Crisis: Little Rock, 1957
*Little Rock Newspapers, Inc.*
http://www.ardemgaz.com/prev/central

A collection of articles and photographs from two Arkansas newspapers explores the 1957 crisis in the city of Little Rock. National attention focused on the city when Governor Orval Faubus refused to allow nine African American students to desegregate the city's all-white Central High School, despite federal court rulings to the contrary. In response, President Dwight D. Eisenhower reluctantly became the first president since Reconstruction to send federal troops to protect the rights of African Americans. Materials include news articles and editorials from each day of the month-long crisis and sixteen photographs. In addition, material on the 40th anniversary of the crisis is provided: thirteen editorials, speeches, an interview with President William J. Clinton, and a 1991 defense by Faubus of his actions.

### 206. CIA Electronic Reading Room
*Central Intelligence Agency (CIA)*
http://www.foia.cia.gov

The Central Intelligence Agency (CIA) has digitized thousands of formerly secret documents declassified to comply with Freedom of Information Act requests. Keyword search capabilities are provided for the complete website. In addition, there are eight collections designated as "frequently requested records" that total more than 7,800 documents. These collections cover a number of Cold War topics: CIA involvement in the 1954 coup in Guatemala; atomic spies Ethel and Julius Rosenberg; the 1961 Bay of Pigs affair; and two well-known espionage incidents. Additional topics include POWs and MIAs in Vietnam, human rights abuses in Latin

Photograph from *Central High Crisis: Little Rock, 1957* [205].
*(Arkansas Democrat Gazette and Will Counts)*

America, and UFOs. The website also offers 896 analytic reports on the Soviet Union produced between 1951 and 1991. Some material, the website notes, cannot be disclosed due to national security laws, and released pages often have material deleted or blacked out. Still, the material offered is voluminous and useful for studying Cold War foreign policy and military history.

### 207. Civil Rights in Mississippi Digital Archive
*University of Southern Mississippi Libraries and Center for Oral History*
http://www.lib.usm.edu/~spcol/crda/oh

These 150 oral history interviews and sixteen collections of documents address the civil rights movement in Mississippi. Interviews were conducted with figures on both sides of the movement. Document collections, donated by volunteers and activists from Mississippi and elsewhere, offer hundreds of pages of letters, journals, photographs, pamphlets, newsletters, FBI documents, and arrest records. Additional documents are being added. Users may browse finding aids for links to digitized materials or search by keyword. Six collections pertain to Freedom Summer, the 1964 volunteer initiative in Mississippi to establish schools, register voters, and organize a biracial Democratic Party. One collection is devoted to the freedom riders who challenged segregation in 1961. Short biographies are furnished on each interviewee and donor, as well as a list of topics addressed and thirty links to other civil rights websites.

### 208. Communism in Washington State — History and Memory Project
*Harry Bridges Center for Labor Studies, University of Washington*
http://faculty.washington.edu/gregoryj/cpproject

A small but well-constructed website on the activities and influence of the Communist Party (CP) in Washington State, where the CP had more significance than in most other areas of the United States. The website contains twenty-one video excerpts of oral history interviews with five current members who describe experiences from the late 1930s to the present. Topics include the role of the CP in 1930s labor organizing, relations with the Soviet Union, the Red Scare that began in 1947, and 1960s antiracism activity. Additional subjects cover relations with the New Left, plans for revitalization, methods of recruitment, and growing up in a Communist family. The website offers nine essays totaling 25,000 words, accompanied by more than 200 images that provide a narrative history of the movement. Users will also find thirty woodcut illustrations from two radical 1930s journals and an annotated timeline. This website provides a good introduction to radical politics on a local level.

### 209. Document Archive of Declassified Files from the Cuban Missile Crisis
*National Security Agency*
http://www.nsa.gov/docs/cuba/archive.htm

On this website, the U.S. National Security Agency (NSA) provides access to facsimiles of 100 declassified documents relating to the Cuban missile crisis. The documents include reports from Signal and Communications Intelligence and NSA memos, twenty written by the director of the NSA. Documents are indexed by date, and each entry includes a ten-word description. The documents describe Soviet involvement in Cuba and Cuban military activities from 1960 to 1963. This website also provides a 2,500-word synopsis of the crisis that recaps events. This is valuable material for studying Cold War history and the NSA's role in the handling of the crisis.

### 210. Experiencing War: Stories from the Veterans History Project
*Library of Congress, American Folklife Center*
http://www.loc.gov/folklife/vets/stories/ex-war-home.html

A collection of video oral histories and additional material — memoirs (some lengthy), letters, diaries, photo albums, scrapbooks, poetry, artwork, and official documents — from American veterans of twentieth-century wars. The website currently provides materials from forty-four veterans, grouped into six thematic categories: courage, patriotism, community, sweethearts, buddies, and family ties. The twenty-five video interviews currently available range from twenty-five minutes to two hours in length. The material presented is part of a rapidly growing archive, the Veterans History Project, created by Congress in 2000 to collect stories from the 19 million veterans presently alive. Ten additional interviews are available from the project's main website: **http://www.loc.gov/folklife/vets/sights-stories.html**. Visitors are encouraged to participate in this project to document veterans' experiences by interviewing relatives, friends, and acquaintances. The materials provide an array of personal views on the American war experience along with visual examples of oral history methods.

### 211. *Foreign Relations of the United States, 1945–1972*
*U.S. State Department*
http://www.state.gov/r/pa/ho/frus

Published annually by the State Department, *Foreign Relations of the United States* (*FRUS*) is the official record of major declassified U.S. foreign policy decisions and diplomatic activity. Material comes from presidential libraries, including transcripts of tape recordings, and executive departments and agencies. Digitized material does not yet reflect the full range of the published volumes. For the Truman administration, the website provides "1945–50, Emergence of the Intelligence Establishment." Three volumes are available for the Eisenhower years: American republics; Guatemala; and Eastern Europe, the Soviet Union, and Cyprus. The Kennedy administration is represented by fifteen volumes that cover, among other areas, Vietnam, the Cuban missile crisis, the Berlin crisis, and exchanges with Soviet Union premier Nikita S. Khrushchev. Thirty-one volumes are available on the Johnson administration, and three volumes are furnished from the Nixon administration. Useful volume summaries provide historical context. *FRUS* volumes for 1900–1918 are available separately [151].

### 212. Historical Atlas of the Twentieth Century
*Matthew White*
http://users.erols.com/mwhite28/20centry.htm

Through a series of maps of countries, continents, and the world, users can trace large-scale demographic, economic, and political trends and developments covering the twentieth century. Topics charted on these maps include changes in the agricultural workforce, infant mortality rates, life expectancy, literacy, persons with telephones, systems of government, alliances, borders between countries, and political violence, including wars. When examining a map, click on buttons to find contextual information from additional maps. The atlas provides a quick and easy way to see comparative change over time on a worldwide basis. The website also includes informative timelines. The site was developed by a librarian for his "own benefit." The categorization scheme does not necessarily reflect the views of professional historians.

### 213. History and Politics Out Loud
*Jerry Goldman, Northwestern University*
http://www.hpol.org

Audio materials on this website were designed to capture "significant political and historical events and personalities of the twentieth century." Materials include 107 items, such as speeches, addresses, and private telephone conversations from nineteen speakers. Most material comes from three U.S. presidents — Richard M. Nixon (thirty-four items); Lyndon Baines Johnson (thirty items); and John F. Kennedy (nineteen items). Additional material comes from international figures such as Secretary of State George Marshall; British prime minister Winston

Churchill; civil rights leaders Martin Luther King Jr. (five items), John Lewis, and A. Philip Randolph; Supreme Court justices William O. Douglas, Arthur J. Goldberg, and Oliver Wendell Holmes Jr.; and Soviet Union premier Nikita S. Khrushchev. This website provides an opportunity to experience the persuasive powers of twentieth-century leaders.

### 214. Internet Moving Images Archive
*Rick Prelinger, Prelinger Archives, and Internet Archive*
http://webdev.archive.org/movies/prelinger.php

This website offers films from a privately held collection of twentieth-century American ephemeral films — produced for short-term purposes and not intended for long-term survival. The website contains more than 2,800 high-quality digital video files documenting various aspects of twentieth-century North American culture, society, leisure, history, industry, technology, and landscape. It includes films produced between 1927 and 1987 by and for U.S. corporations, nonprofit organizations, trade associations, community and interest groups, and educational institutions. More than fifty films pertain to Cold War issues. Films depict ordinary people in normal daily activities, such as working, dishwashing, driving, and learning proper behavior, in addition to treating such subjects as education, health, immigration, nuclear energy, social issues, and religion. The website contains an index of 403 categories. This is an important source for studying business history, advertising, cinema studies, the Cold War, and twentieth-century American cultural history.

### 215. Jazz: A Film by Ken Burns
*PBS Interactive*
http://www.pbs.org/jazz

A companion to a PBS documentary series, this website offers information on the history of jazz and audio samples. The website is divided into three main sections. *Places, Spaces, and Changing Faces* describes the cities and clubs — in New Orleans, Chicago, New York, and Kansas City — and the migrations of African Americans from the South and immigrants from Europe that contributed to the growth of jazz. *Jazz Lounge* outlines basic characteristics of jazz rhythm and melody and describes seven major strains of development from New Orleans style to free jazz and fusion. *Jazz in Time* places the music within a changing historical context. Links offer more than 100 biographies of musicians and close to 100 audio clips of music and interviews. About twenty of the interviews are transcribed. A virtual piano in the *Jazz Lounge* provides an interactive opportunity to learn about and practice basic jazz techniques.

### 216. Literature and Culture of the American 1950s
*Al Filreis, University of Pennsylvania*
http://dept.english.upenn.edu/~afilreis/50s/home.html

More than 100 primary texts, essays, biographical sketches, obituaries, book reviews, and partially annotated links explore the cultural, intellectual, and political trends of the 1950s. Organized alphabetically and according to lesson plans, this eclectic collection of readings is structured around a few landmark texts and topics, including McCarthyism and anticommunism, Daniel Bell's *The End of Ideology* (1960), William H. Whyte's *The Organization Man* (1956), feminism, Philip Rieff's *The Triumph of the Therapeutic* (1966), and conformity in universities. Materials include substantial excerpts from Vance Packard's *The Status Seekers* (1959) and the *Encyclopedia of the American Left*, in addition to retrospective analyses of the postwar period.

### 217. Lyndon Baines Johnson Library and Museum

*Lyndon Baines Johnson Library and Museum*
http://www.lbjlib.utexas.edu

The heart of this collection about President Lyndon Baines Johnson is a group of seventy-seven oral history interviews (35 to 200 pages each) with members of his administration, congressional colleagues, journalists, civil rights leaders, and a historian. The website provides fourteen audio files, including telephone conversations, State of the Union addresses, Johnson's speech to Congress following the Kennedy assassination, and an excerpt of his television address announcing his decision not to run for a second term. Also available are transcripts of twenty-five speeches; forty days of diary entries; the ninety-nine National Security Action memoranda issued during his presidency relaying foreign policy directives and initiating actions; and 150 photographs. Biographical information is furnished in two chronologies. An exhibit from the Johnson museum provides an essay about events in Johnson's lifetime.

### 218. Martin Luther King Jr. Papers Project

*Stanford University*
http://www.stanford.edu/group/King

Featuring texts by and about Martin Luther King Jr., this regularly updated website currently contains approximately 400 speeches, sermons, and other writings, mostly taken from four volumes covering the period from 1929 to 1958. These are listed in the *Published Documents* section under "Papers." In addition, sixteen chapters of materials published in *The Autobiography of Martin Luther King Jr.* are available. The website presents important sermons and speeches from later periods, including "Letter from a Birmingham Jail," the March on Washington address, the Nobel Peace Prize acceptance speech, and "Beyond Vietnam." Additional materials include an interactive chronology of King's life; a biographical essay; twenty-three audio files of recorded speeches and sermons; twelve articles on King; and thirty-two photographs. This website is valuable for studying King's views and discourse on civil rights, race relations, nonviolence, education, peace, and other political, religious, and philosophical topics.

### 219. National Election Studies

*National Election Studies, Center for Political Studies,*
*University of Michigan*
http://www.umich.edu/~nes

This website contains a wealth of data from National Election Studies, which produces "high quality data on voting, public opinion, and political participation" and surveys of the American electorate conducted in presidential and congressional election years from 1948 to 2002. Large files of raw data can be downloaded, but these are designed to be used by social science professionals. For students of political and social history, *The NES Guide to Public Opinion and Electoral Behavior* will be useful. Composed of more than 200 tables and graphs, the guide traces nine key variables in the makeup and opinions of the electorate from 1948 to 2002: social and religious characteristics; partisanship and evaluation of political parties; ideological self-identification; public opinion on public policy issues; support for the political system; political involvement and partisanship; evaluation of presidential candidates; evaluation of congressional candidates; and vote choice. This website also provides pilot studies on recent surveying issues, such as properly measuring exposure to television ads and defining "social trust."

### 220. Parallel History Project on NATO and the Warsaw Pact
*Vojtech Mastny, Project Coordinator*
http://www.isn.ethz.ch/php

This website currently provides approximately 350 recently declassified documents from archives of former Warsaw Pact countries and the United States that reveal previously hidden aspects of Cold War military strategy. The project offers documents and accompanying analyses in six categories: Warsaw Pact records; Warsaw Pact war plans; NATO (North Atlantic Treaty Organization) records (U.S. and British); national perspectives (Bulgaria, Romania, Hungary, China, and Poland); crises (Berlin and Libya); and intelligence. The website also provides thirteen oral history interviews with former officials, including two Eisenhower administration officers involved with NATO planning and nuclear weapons policies. Documents reveal a 1964 Warsaw Pact war plan for using nuclear weapons in a preemptive strike against NATO forces, and a 1965 Hungarian army exercise detailing the targeted destruction of Western European cities, including Vienna, Munich, Verona, and Vicenza. A thirty-page survey article assesses history written since the release of recent documents.

### 221. Ripple of Hope in the Land of Apartheid: Robert Kennedy in South Africa, June 4–9, 1966
*Larry Shore, Hunter College*
http://www.rfksa.org

Senator Robert F. Kennedy's trip to South Africa in June 1966 to protest apartheid and support efforts to combat it is amply documented on this website with texts, audio files, film clips, and photographs. Texts of the five speeches delivered by Kennedy during the visit are available, and full audio files are provided for three. The website also offers texts of ten additional speeches (with four audio files) from South African students and political leaders, as well as American leaders. There are twenty-eight related documents, including United Nations documents and a *Look* magazine article written by the senator; twenty-two photographs; twenty-one political cartoons; and three film clips. An overview describes the "enormous impact" of Kennedy's visit and illuminates "the manner in which he subtly challenged and undermined some of the pillars of apartheid ideology and mythology." A valuable website for studying the history of race relations in South Africa and the United States.

### 222. Truman Presidential Museum and Library
*Harry S. Truman Library*
http://www.trumanlibrary.org/library.htm

The presidency of Harry S. Truman is addressed through this archive of hundreds of government documents. Materials are organized into twelve central areas: the Berlin airlift; the decision to drop the atomic bomb; desegregation of the Armed Forces; the election campaign of 1948; Korean War; Marshall Plan; NATO; the Truman Doctrine; Truman's Farewell Address; recognition of the State of Israel; United Nations; and the incarceration of Japanese Americans during World War II. Transcripts are available for approximately 120 oral histories conducted with members of Truman's administration and officials from other countries about the Korean War. The website also offers the full text of Truman's diary from 1947; twenty audio files with extracts of speeches, press conferences, and interviews; 122 biographical photographs; and thirty-four political cartoons. This is a rich resource for exploring international relations in the early postwar era.

### 223. U.S. Senate Historical Office
*U.S. Senate Historical Office*
http://www.senate.gov/learning/learn_history.html

This collection of oral histories, essays, and data addresses the history of the U.S. Senate. Complete texts of nineteen oral histories (40 to 600 pages) of retired staff and one senator cover the years from 1910 to 1984 and deal with the workings of the Senate. Issues discussed include desegregation of staff, the McCarthy hearings, preparations to impeach Nixon, and the impact of computers. The website also provides an overview of Senate history; more than 140 "historical minutes" relating significant issues and events; a collection of twenty-six essays on Senate procedure, leadership, and officers; a biographical directory; and statistical information and tables. The minutes of Senate Republican Conferences (1911 to 1964) and Democratic Conferences (1903 to 1964) are available, as are eight lectures by statesmen in the Leaders Lectures series established in 1988.

### 224. Vietnam Center
*Vietnam Center, Texas Tech University*
http://www.ttu.edu/~vietnam

This massive website offers 234 audio oral histories (120 have been transcribed) with U.S. men and women who served in Vietnam. In addition, more than 545,000 pages from more than 63,000 documents regarding the Vietnam War are available in the *Virtual Vietnam Archive*, which also offers video interviews. The website focuses on military and diplomatic history but aims to record the experiences of ordinary individuals involved in Vietnam and on the home front. Additional items address Thailand, Laos, and Cambodia, as well as Americans and Vietnamese. Secondary and reference resources are also available, including conference papers, text and video versions of a 1996 address by former ambassador William Colby on "Turning Points in the Vietnam War," and links to twenty related websites.

**225. Women in Journalism**

*Washington Press Club Foundation*

http://npc.press.org/wpforal/ohhome.htm

This website provides access to forty-one "full-life" interviews of American women journalists that compose the oral history project of the Washington Press Club Foundation. The collection includes interviews with women who began their careers in the 1920s and continues to the present. Print, radio, and television journalism all are represented. Interviews address difficulties women have encountered entering the profession and how their presence has changed the field. The website introduces the oral histories with a 1,000-word preface and an explanation of the methodology of the website. Each interview is linked to a photograph and a 100-word biographical sketch of the interviewee. Interviews range from one to twelve sessions, and each session is about twenty pages long. The interviews are indexed but are not searchable by subject. This is a valuable resource for studying women's history and the history of journalism.

## Contemporary United States, 1968 to the Present

**226. AIDS at 20**

New York Times

http://www.nytimes.com/library/national/
science/aids/aids-index.html

More than 350 *New York Times* articles from 1981 to 2001 related to the AIDS epidemic are available on this website. Materials include nine articles specifically related to the course of the epidemic's devastation in Africa. There are nine videos, six multimedia presentations, five fact sheets, and four in-depth reports on such subjects as H.I.V. medications, AIDS in New York City, H.I.V. and teens, women and AIDS, the federal response to the crisis, and the history of AIDS.

**227. Bureau of Economic Analysis**

*U.S. Department of Commerce, Economics and Statistics Administration*
http://www.bea.doc.gov

Comprehensive and summary data estimates are available concerning national, international, and regional economic activity. Additional data are available according to industry. An overview of the economy provides data on production, purchases by type, prices, personal income, government finances, inventories, and balance of payments. An easy-to-use keyword index to a set of annual and quarterly national income and product account (NIPA) tables from 1929 to 2002 — found in the *National* section under "Personal Income and Outlays" — allows users access to data on specific product sales and ways that consumers have spent money. Recent research papers by staff members address subjects such as globalization, how the "new economy" is measured, and structural change of the economy over the past twenty-four years.

## 228. Centennial Celebration

*Bureau of the Census*
http://www.census.gov/mso/www/centennial

This website provides a wealth of U.S. statistical population data. In addition to recent data, there are more than thirty comprehensive reports and tables that track demographic shifts by decade, including urban and rural population change, population of the largest 100 cities, population density, and homeownership rates. Additional materials detail shifts in U.S. international trade; poverty; race and Hispanic origin of foreign-born populations; interracial married couples; and marital status of women at first birth. Visitors can find detailed information on business sectors as well as the social and economic characteristics of African Americans, Hispanics and Latinos, Asians and Pacific Islanders, American Indian and Alaska Natives, and baby boomers. In addition, the website provides recent demographic data, a collection of "fast facts" for each decade of the twentieth century, and four historical timelines.

## 229. ECHO: Exploring and Collecting History Online—Science and Technology

*Center for History and New Media, George Mason University*
http://chnm.gmu.edu/echo

ECHO is designed to promote and improve the history of science and technology on the web. ECHO offers a directory that collects, categorizes, and reviews existing sites on the history of science and technology and consults with historians who wish to explore the unique ways the Internet can aid and expand their work. The project also reaches out to those who experienced the scientific and technological advances and setbacks of the twentieth century with a Memory Bank of more than 800 firsthand accounts. ECHO's directory of history of science websites has 2,700 entries. Roughly 500 of these are annotated, and the rest offer brief excerpts from the sites. Sub-projects cover the history of space exploration and computing, the role of women in the sciences and engineering, and the impact of technology on postwar America.

## 230. Economic Data, Fred II

*Federal Reserve Bank of St. Louis*
http://www.stls.frb.org/fred

These statistical data document national economic and financial trends in twelve broad categories: business/fiscal; commercial banking; consumer price indexes; employment and population; exchange rate, balance of payments, and trade data; gross domestic product and components; interest rates; monetary aggregates; producer price indexes; reserves; regional (covering Arkansas, Illinois, Indiana, Kentucky, Mississippi, Missouri, and Tennessee), including employment and banking data; and U.S. financial data. Most of the data, prepared by the Federal Reserve Bank of St. Louis Research Division to aid in economic policy decisions, were compiled monthly to track shifting trends. Charts that track trends in employment, unemployment, salary, and retail sales according to economic sector and state are especially valuable. Trends are charted in time frames of five-year, ten-year, or "max" (which can go back to 1901).

### 231. Freedom of Information Act, Electronic Reading Room
*Federal Bureau of Investigation*
http://foia.fbi.gov/room.htm

Thousands of documents from more than 150 FBI files, declassified due to Freedom of Information Act requests, are available here. Many documents have been heavily censored and are barely legible. Cases include the Sacco-Vanzetti case in the 1920s; the 1932 Bonus March; the Black Legion of the 1930s; the Young Communist League, 1939 to 1941; the *Daily Worker* in the late 1940s and 1950s; the murder of three civil rights workers in Mississippi in 1964; SNCC, beginning in 1964; the Ku Klux Klan in 1964 and 1965; a Black Panther Party chapter beginning in 1969; the Watergate break-in of 1972; the white hate group Posse Comitas in 1973; the Weather Underground in the 1970s; and the Gay Activists Alliance of the 1970s.

### 232. Gulf War
*Frontline, Public Broadcasting System*
http://www.pbs.org/wgbh/pages/frontline/gulf

This companion website offers material on Operation Desert Storm, emphasizing the perspectives of those directly involved. There are nineteen oral history interviews (up to twenty pages each) with eight "decision makers," seven commanders, two Iraqi officials, and two news analysts. *War Stories*, personal reminiscences of five pilots, are available in text and audio. *Weapons and Technology* details munitions and ten ground, aircraft, and space weapons systems. A seven-minute video excerpt is available from the *Frontline* program, as are four fifteen-minute episodes of a BBC radio program in text and audio. The website includes a chronology, ten maps, a bibliography, facts and statistics, and brief essays on press coverage and Iraqi war deaths. Links are available to five websites produced to accompany more recent *Frontline* reports on Iraq.

### 233. Hard Hat Riots: An Online History Project
*Karl Miller, Ellen Noonan, and John Spencer*
http://chnm.gmu.edu/hardhats/homepage.html

This well-designed website presents multiple perspectives on the May 8, 1970, attacks in New York City on Vietnam War protesters by hundreds of construction workers. Users can enter the website by selecting any of twelve photographs, nine newspaper headlines, or three websites in the city where rioting occurred, or by following one of ten summaries by historians and journalists. Selected items link to additional resources, including a police report and interviews with a student and a construction worker. The creators challenge users to fit the riots into wider contexts and to assess varying attempts at historical understanding. Though limited in scope, this website is useful for studying social class in the Vietnam War era, labor history, and media influence in American life.

### 234. Herblock's History: Political Cartoons from the Crash to the Millennium
*Library of Congress*
http://www.loc.gov/rr/print/swann/herblock

This exhibit presents 135 cartoons drawn between 1929 and 2000 by three-time Pulitzer Prize–winning political cartoonist Herblock (Herbert Block). Cartoons comment on major events and public issues. The website also presents an essay by Block on "the cartoon as an opinion medium"; a biographical essay; and fifteen caricatures of the cartoonist by well-known colleagues. Cartoons are organized according to thirteen chronological sections, with an additional segment devoted to U.S. presidents. Brief annotations provide historical context for each image. A tribute website by the *Washington Post*, Herblock's longtime employer, offers additional cartoons and essays by Block **(http://www.washingtonpost.com/wp-srv/metro/specials/herblock)**.

### 235. Inter-University Consortium for Political and Social Research
*Institute for Social Research, University of Michigan*
http://www.icpsr.umich.edu    $ $

This website provides access to social science data for member colleges and universities. Data offered cover a range of sociological and political areas, including census enumerations; urban and community studies; conflict, violence, and wars; economic behavior; legal systems; legislative bodies; mass political behavior and attitudes; and organizational behavior. Although much of the website emphasizes the late twentieth century, data sets such as "Historical and Contemporary Electoral Processes" and "1790–1960 Censuses" are useful for historical research. Searching

Cartoon from *Herblock's History* [234].
*(© 2000 by Herblock in* The Washington Post*)*

is available according to a controlled vocabulary of names, subjects, and geographical terms. There are ten special topic archives with data on health, education, aging, criminal justice, and substance abuse and mental health concerns. A "data use tutorial" and links to related websites may be useful.

### 236. Legacy Tobacco Documents Library
*University of California, San Francisco Library; American*
*Legacy Foundation*
http://legacy.library.ucsf.edu

This website provides more than 38 million pages of tobacco industry documents. Documents were made public as a stipulation of the 1998 Master Settlement Agreement to settle multiple lawsuits. Index records, prepared by tobacco companies, can be searched; full-text searching is not available. Documents range from the 1930s to the 1990s, although most were created since the 1950s and deal with industry concerns such as marketing, sales, advertising, research and development, manufacturing, and expansion of business to developing countries. There are eighty links to related websites and promises to include more documents in the future. Although not particularly user-friendly, this website offers an abundance of material for studying the history of smoking, advertising, and twentieth-century American business practices.

### 237. Legal Foundation for Hawaiian Independence
*Legal Foundation for Hawaiian Independence*
http://www.hawaii-nation.org/legal.html

This website presents documents in support of the movement for Hawaiian sovereignty, begun in earnest following the 1993 "Apology Resolution" passed by Congress and signed by President William J. Clinton. Documents include five constitutions of the Kingdom of Hawaii from 1840 to 1893; an 1843 declaration by the United Kingdom and France recognizing its independence; fourteen treaties made with Hawaii between 1827 and 1887; six documents about overthrow and annexation; three about the territorial era between 1900 and 1950; the Statehood Admissions Act, the legality of which is addressed; and material on the "Apology Resolution" and independence movement. These documents are part of a larger website that includes newspaper coverage of the movement. This is valuable for researching the history of Hawaii and American imperialism.

### 238. Living Room Candidate: A History of Presidential Campaign Commercials, 1952–2000
*American Museum of the Moving Image*
http://www.ammi.org/livingroomcandidate

These 183 television commercials appeared since 1952 to sell presidential candidates to the American public. The website also provides an annotated guide to twenty-one websites created for the 1996 and 2000 elections. Ads from each election are accessible by year as well as by common themes and strategies used over the years, such as "Looking Presidential," "Attack Ads," "Family Man," and "Real

People." Essays focus on analyzing ad strategies of major party candidates, and a program guide offers a history of the usage of television commercials in campaigns.

### 239. Living Voices, Voces Vivas
*Smithsonian National Museum of the American Indian*
http://www.nmai.si.edu/livingvoices

This website provides audio files of forty American Indians and Native Hawaiians discussing their diverse experiences, histories, and traditions, with an emphasis on current concerns and projects. Those interviewed come from Canada, Mexico, and Panama, in addition to various parts of the United States. Interviewees include artists, writers, musicians, teachers, scientists, activists, tribal leaders, students, scholars, religious leaders, a gaming establishment head, an illusionist, a former Miss Indian World, and the head of an organization dedicated to preserving indigenous traditions. The website is divided into English- and Spanish-language sections. Each talk lasts from three to five minutes; some talks are translated into English or Spanish. Access to the interviews is provided through a "Flash website" to accommodate high-speed connections and an HTML website for slower modems. The latter includes interview transcripts.

### 240. Making the Macintosh: Technology and Culture in Silicon Valley
*Alex Soojung-Kim Pang, Stanford University Library*
http://library.stanford.edu/mac

This website is devoted to the history of the Macintosh computer. Rather than profile Apple Computer's leader, Steve Jobs, and well-publicized software and hardware developers, materials include thirteen interviews with designers, technical writers, Apple employees, the organizer of a Berkeley user group, and a San Francisco journalist who covered early developments. In addition, more than seventy documents from the late 1970s to the present chart company and user group developments, beginning with roots in the 1960s counterculture philosophy. Documents include "From Satori to Silicon Valley," a lecture by Theodore Roszak first delivered in 1985 with afterthoughts added in 2000; thirteen texts by the first Mac designer, Jef Raskin; press releases and other marketing materials; and texts relating to user groups. More than 100 images include patent drawings and product photographs.

### 241. Multilaterals Project
*Fletcher School of Law and Diplomacy, Tufts University*
http://fletcher.tufts.edu/multilaterals.html

Texts of more than 260 international multilateral treaties, agreements, and conventions are available on this website, from the Treaty of Westphalia (1648) to the International Code of Conduct on the Distribution and Use of Pesticides (November 2002). Originally designed to provide environmental agreements, this website now offers additional texts, including drafts. Materials are arranged according to ten categories: atmosphere and space; flora and fauna, biodiversity; cultural protection; diplomatic relations; general; human rights; marine and coastal; other environmental; trade and commercial relations; and rules of warfare and arms control. Most of the texts date from the post–World War II period to the present. Listings are arranged in chronological order, and users may search by keyword. There are links to approximately 120 additional sources for treaties and conventions.

### 242. National Security Archive
*Thomas S. Blanton, Director*
http://www.gwu.edu/~nsarchiv

Despite its official-sounding name, this is a nongovernmental institution. Founded in 1985 as a central repository for declassified materials obtained through Freedom of Information Act requests, the *Archive* offers 100 "Electronic Briefing Books," each providing government documents and a contextual narrative on national security history and issues, foreign policy initiatives, and military history. Although much of the material relates to events abroad, documents provide information on U.S. involvement and perceptions. Major categories include Europe (Hungarian Revolution, Solidarity, and the 1989 revolutions); Latin America (overall CIA involvement, war in Colombia, contras, Mexico); nuclear history (treaties, Berlin crisis, India and Pakistan, North Korea, China, Israel); Middle East and South Asia (Iraq and WMD, hostages in Iran, October 1973 war); the U.S. intelligence community; government secrecy; humanitarian interventions; and September 11 sourcebooks on the terrorist threat. A companion, subscription-based site (http://nsarchive .chadwyck.com) offers more than 40,000 of the most important declassified documents regarding U.S. policy.

### 243. Oral History Digital Collection
*Center for Historic Preservation, William F. Maag Jr. Library,*
*Youngstown State University*
http://www.maag.ysu.edu/oralhistory/oral_hist.html

This website provides full-text, first-person narratives for 1,100 people from northeast Ohio on issues significant to the state and the nation. These oral histories, collected since 1974, focus on topics such as ethnic culture (African American, Greek, Irish, Italian, Jewish, Puerto Rican, Romanian, and Russian), industry (steel, pottery, brick, coal, and railroads), labor relations (including women in labor unions), wars (World War II, Vietnam, Gulf War), college life (including the shootings by National Guard troops at Kent State in 1970), the Holocaust, and religion. Subject access is available through more than 200 topics listed alphabetically.

### 244. Oyez: U.S. Supreme Court Multimedia
*Jerry Goldman, Northwestern University*
http://oyez.itcs.northwestern.edu/oyez/frontpage

These audio files, abstracts, transcriptions of oral arguments, and written opinions cover more than 3,300 Supreme Court cases. Materials include 2,000 hours, in audio, of arguments in selected cases starting in 1955 and all cases since 1995. Users can access cases through keyword searches or a list of fourteen broad categories, including civil rights, due process, First Amendment, judicial power, privacy, and unions. Easy access is available to the twenty "most popular cases," determined by numbers of hits. These include *Roe* v. *Wade* (abortion), *Gideon* v. *Wainwright* (right to counsel), *Plessy* v. *Ferguson* (segregation), *Grutter* v. *Bollinger* (racial preferences in school admissions decisions), and *Bush* v. *Gore* (election results). Biographies are provided for all Court justices, and *The Pending Docket* provides briefs and additional materials on upcoming cases. The website also includes links to written opinions since 1893.

### 245. *Public Papers of the Presidents of the United States, 1992–2001*

*National Archives and Records Administration, Office of the Federal Register*
**http://www.gpo.gov/nara/pubpaps/photoidx.html**

These digitized versions of twenty volumes of *Public Papers of the Presidents of the United States* span 1992 to 2001. Material includes papers and speeches issued by the Office of the Press Secretary during the terms of William J. Clinton (seventeen volumes, 1993 to 2001), in addition to two volumes pertaining to George H. W. Bush for 1992, and one volume for George W. Bush (January 20–June 30, 2001). The documents, including addresses, statements, letters, and interviews with the press, are compiled by the Office of the Federal Register and published in chronological order. Also included are appendixes with daily schedules and meetings, nominations to the Senate, proclamations, and executive orders. Users may access multiple volumes by keyword searches and separate volumes by title of document, type, subject matter, and personal names.

Photograph of President Clinton in India at *Public Papers of the Presidents of the United States, 1992–2001* [245].
*(Government Printing Office)*

### 246. SDA: Survey Documentation and Analysis
*University of California, Berkeley*
http://sda.berkeley.edu:7502

Within this website designed for social science researchers conducting quantitative studies, historians can find material relating to trends and shifts in American attitudes and opinions. Topics include surveys on race and politics, labor, health issues, and voter attitudes since 1952. Perhaps most valuable is the General Social Survey, an "almost annual" study since 1972 that interviewed U.S. households about attitudes on an eclectic range of topics related to public policy. Data include beliefs concerning welfare, free speech, gun control, class structure, pornography, race, religion, media exposure, working mothers, and women's rights. Since 1982, surveys in other countries have replicated questions so cross-national analyses may be conducted.

### 247. September 11 Digital Archive
*Center for History and New Media, George Mason University, and*
*American Social History Project, City University of New York*
http://www.911digitalarchive.org

This archive uses electronic media to collect, preserve, and present the history and memory of the September 11, 2001, attacks in New York, Virginia, and Pennsylvania, as well as the public responses to them. The *Digital Archive* collects firsthand accounts of the attacks and the aftermath, archives emails and digital images growing out of the events, organizes and annotates the most important web-based resources on the subject, and develops materials to contextualize and teach about these events. There are more than 130,000 digital objects, including 12,000 recollections and images currently available, as well as annotations for almost 400 websites related to September 11, 2001, including online memorials, document archives, and government and personal sites. In addition, the archive presents forty-seven relevant reports, nearly 300 audio recordings, four video presentations, and a flyer collection of nearly 1,000 posters, press releases, brochures, newsletters, events programs, and other related material present on New York City streets in the year following the attacks.

### 248. Teach Women's History Project
*Feminist Majority Foundation*
http://www.feminist.org/research/teach1.html

These teaching and reference materials address the women's rights movement of the past fifty years and opposing forces. Materials include forty primary documents selected from *The Feminist Chronicles: 1953–1993*, ranging from the first National Organization for Women (NOW) statement of purpose to topical task force statements. There are thirty suggestions for further reading in women's history, feminist theory, and contemporary women's issues, as well as listings for nineteen relevant organizations. The *Feminist Internet Gateway* provides forty annotated links in "Women's History and Education Resources," as well as links to contemporary topics.

### 249. Watergate Revisited

*Washington Post*

http://www.washingtonpost.com/wp-srv/national/longterm/
watergate/splash1a.htm

This is a thorough introduction to the Watergate scandal. Created by the *Washington Post*, the newspaper whose investigative journalism led to President Richard M. Nixon's downfall, the website provides more than eighty relevant news stories. It also offers links to thirty-seven online documents — speeches, tape transcriptions, and Nixon's letter of resignation — in the National Archives and Nixon Library. A detailed timeline links to *Post* stories, and brief biographies introduce twenty-four "key players" in various phases of the scandal. Users may view four video clips of Nixon's "I am not a crook" speech, Nixon's announcement of his resignation, a farewell to his staff, and John Dean's testimony. The *Post*'s Bob Woodward and Ben Bradlee discuss the scandal in a video recording of a 2002 forum and the transcript of a 1997 interview. The website also includes a link to cartoons by Herblock, audio files, and photographs.

### 250. WTO History Project

*University of Washington*

http://depts.washington.edu/wtohist

Designed to provide access to documents by groups that protested the World Trade Organization's "Ministerial Week," held in Seattle from November 29 to December 3, 1999. Texts include eighty oral histories of organizers and participants, seventy-three photographs, and images of 224 flyers, posters, and leaflets. Additional materials include forty-six planning documents, eighteen signs, two audio files, three videos, and two timelines. Documents can be searched by keyword, organization, and issues, such as labor, environment, trade, democracy, direct action, food, agriculture, health, and independent media.

# Using Search Engines Effectively

Google is by far the most popular search engine. But there is a lot more to using this powerful tool than simply entering a few keywords and pressing "Search." Here are some tips on getting the most out of your internet searching.

## Use Advanced Search

The easiest way to go from thousands of pages that seem irrelevant to a few useful pages is to use the Advanced Search feature. You can click on "Advanced Search" from the main search page or go directly to **http://www.google .com/advanced_search**.

## Enter More Than One Term

If you are interested in the role played by American troops in the Boxer Rebellion, you'll want to enter *boxer rebellion American troops* because anything else might take you to a site on Muhammad Ali!

## Use Quotation Marks

Using quotation marks helps to keep two search terms together. So if you are researching the Seaman's Act of 1916, your search term will be *"Seaman's Act"* 1916. Searching for *Captain Absolom Boston* returns 414 mostly irrelevant sites. Searching for *"Captain Absolom Boston"* reduces that number to a single site about black whalers that contains a picture of the Nantucket native.

## Tell Google Where to Find It

Suppose you know that you saw a page about John Malcom, the British customs officer at Boston during the Townshend initiatives, at the free online encyclopedia **wikipedia.org**, but you don't remember anything else. You can search *"John Malcom" site:wikipedia.org*. If you remember that the title of the site you want is *The Black Military Experience,* you can type *intitle: "Black Military Experience"* to get right to the site. Here is a list of operators to use to fine-tune a search:

    intext:
    allintext:
    allintitle:
    inurl:

author:
location:
site:
intitle:

## Use the '+', '−' , '|', and '~' Signs

If you are interested in the role of women in World War I and President Wilson, you might search for *"Woodrow Wilson"* + *"World War I"* + *Women*. To find out about the Mercury Capsule but not about its 1999 recovery off the ocean floor, type *"Mercury Capsule"* − *recovery*. The symbol '|' basically means "or," so if you are searching for information on the John Scopes trial, you might try *"John Scopes"* | *monkey* because the trial was also called the "Monkey" trial. If you aren't sure about different names for the same thing, you can try using the '~' symbol: *~cherokee* as opposed to *cherokee* will double the number of Google results.

## Translate a Text

Though a rough translator at best, Google can give you the gist of an article in French, German, Spanish, Portuguese, or Italian. See **http://www.google .com/language_tools** for this feature. Be aware, however, that the translations are often imperfect.

## Other Searches

You can get a map of a place by typing an address into Google. You can find out how popular a website is by seeing how many places link to that website. To see how many websites link to another website, you can use the "link:" operator. You can find out what a word means by asking Google. For example, you can find out the two possible meanings of "portmanteau" by entering *define:portmanteau*. You can convert measurements or make a calculation with Google. If you type *"9000/4"* in Google, you'll get "2250." If you type *"35 degrees Celsius in Fahrenheit,"* you'll get "95 degrees Fahrenheit."

## Other Search Engines

Google works by searching for websites that are referenced by other websites. Since every website's author and every organization knows this fact and hopes that their website appears first when individuals enter certain search terms, the Google search engine is frequently deceived and is not always the best way to find reliable information. When searching for information on current events, for example, you should consider skipping Google and searching directly from media websites, such as those of the *New York Times* (**www.nytimes.com**) or the

British Broadcasting System **(www.bbc.co.uk)**, that have broad coverage on current events. You should also consider keeping a library of "favorites" or "bookmarks" of sites that you use frequently for research. You can also try other search engines such as Metacrawler **(www.metacrawler.com)** and Vivísimo **(www.vivisimo.com)**.

An important thing to remember is that even with all these online archives, there is no electronic substitute for traditional research skills. Know what you are looking for, and ask a librarian for advice when you are not sure if you are searching for the right terms.

Using Google's Advanced Search page can save a lot of time otherwise spent sorting through irrelevant or useless sites.
*(Google © 2004)*

# A Glossary of Common Internet Terms

A more extensive glossary may be found at: **http://www.matisse.net/files/ glossary.html**.

**Attachment:** A document, photo, or other file that is sent via electronic mail. Users can download the attachment to read or view it. A writing assignment, for example, can be sent as an attachment.

**Blog:** Short for "web log," a recent phenomenon on the Internet, where blog "authors" publish their ideas, rants, or raves on their personal websites.

**Bookmark:** A browser function that "saves" a website's location for easy return later on; also called "favorite."

**Browser:** Computer software that allows the computer to present World Wide Web (www) sites to the viewer as text and multimedia. Netscape and Internet Explorer are two common browsers.

**Chat:** Synchronous communication between computers on the Internet using voice, video, or plain text. Common chat interfaces include Yahoo! Messenger, IRC, and Windows Messenger.

**Cookie:** A document stored on your computer's hard disk that allows websites to see which sites you go to and when. A cookie also stores information about you so that a website "remembers" you when you return.

**Database:** A searchable and organized repository of information.

**Dead link:** A URL or web address to a site that no longer exists.

**Digitize:** To take something that is in a nondigital format, such as an audiocassette recording or a photograph, and turn it into a digital format for distribution on computers or the Internet.

**DNS:** "Domain Name System." Translates domain names into the computer-readable numerical IP address of each machine on the Internet.

**Domain name:** The domain name is a text name corresponding to the numeric address (see IP address) of a computer. The domain name of the site located at **http://www.loc.gov/exhibits/gadd/4403.html** is "loc.gov."

**Download:** To take a file that resides on one computer on the Internet and move it to another, usually smaller, computer.

**ejournal:** A journal published on the Internet.

**email:** Electronic mail. Notes, memos, and letters that can be sent from one person to another by using an email address.

**email address:** An electronic address for sending email in the format **username@host.domain**.

**ezine:** A magazine published on the Internet.

**FAQ:** "Frequently Asked Questions." A question-and-answer forum, usually about a particular website or its topic.

**Form:** A web page that requests information from the user.

**FTP:** "File Transfer Protocol." A common method of moving files ("downloading" and "uploading") from one computer to another.

**GIF:** "Graphics Interchange Format." A file format used for graphics on the Internet; it allows browsers to display graphics.

**Hit:** Each occurrence of a user accessing a website. The popularity of websites is generally measured in "hits per day."

**Home page:** The web page that serves as the starting point or table of contents for a website; also, a personal website in its entirety.

**Host:** A computer that holds the web page and is connected to the Internet so that other users (called "clients") can access it; also called "server."

**HTML:** "Hypertext Markup Language." The basic code in which most web pages are written.

**HTTP:** "Hypertext Transport Protocol." The method in which web pages are sent from the host to the user's browser.

**Hypertext:** Digitally formatted text that contains hyperlinks.

**Hyperlink:** Text that the user can click to go to another document or part of a website; also called "link."

**Icon:** A graphic symbol on which the user can click to go to another document or part of a website.

**Internet:** A worldwide network of networks in which computers ("clients") communicate with servers ("hosts") or other computers using a variety of methods and for a variety of purposes, including accessing pages on the World Wide Web (www) or email.

**IP address:** "Internet Protocol" address. An address for a computer, analogous to a telephone number, where a server or other computers can find the computer in order to send data to it.

**Java:** A computer language used widely on the Internet to make sophisticated applications capable of producing animations, calculations, or database functions.

**JPEG:** "Joint Photographic Experts Group." A file format used for graphics on the Internet; it allows browsers to display graphics.

**Keyword:** Used in Internet searching, any word that is likely to appear on a website or that sums up part or all of the content of a particular website.

**Link:** See "Hyperlink."

**Listserv:** An email discussion group or its mailing list.

**Login:** As a verb, to access a site using a login name and a password (sometimes called "logging on"). As a noun, the pseudonym used to access a website.

**Mailing list:** An electronic mailing list by which an electronic newsletter or updates are sent to the email addresses of many individuals.

**Mirror:** Websites that are exact replicates of an original website but are hosted elsewhere; a mirror is used to prevent congestion or too many hits on one website.

**Modem:** A device used by a computer to turn digital signals into analog signals to be sent over a phone line to another computer.

**MPEG:** "Motion Picture Experts Group." A standard format for audio and video files frequently found on the Internet.

**MP3:** Based on MPEG technology, this is a file format for high-quality audio.

**Netiquette:** Proper and appropriate behavior on the Internet.

**Netizen:** An involved member of the Internet community, such as someone who has a blog or regularly posts (writes and publishes) opinions on websites.

**Newsgroup:** An electronic forum for discussing a particular topic where queries and responses are posted to a site.

**Online:** Originally meaning that someone was logged in to a particular service and thus "online," it now describes anything that resides on the Internet.

**Password:** A secret, personal code used to access a computer account. Most users set their own passwords.

**PDF:** "Portable Document Format." A common format for sharing formatted documents over the Internet. Users need the free Adobe Acrobat software in order to view the document.

**Posting:** A comment or article written by a user on a blog site or newsgroup.

**QuickTime VR:** A format for viewing a three-dimensional or panoramic view of something.

**Search engine:** A function of a website that allows searches for items on that website. Some websites, such as Altavista and Google, are search engines for many websites.

**Server:** See "Host."

**Spider:** A computer program that maps or finds all the web pages at a certain website.

**Subscription site:** A website that requires a monthly or annual contribution in order to access its content.

**Streaming media:** Audio or video that "streams" continuously through a player such as Real Audio or Windows Media Player instead of first requiring a download.

**TCP/IP:** "Transmission Control Protocol/Internet Protocol." The group of universal formats by which computers transmit and receive data on the Internet.

**Upload:** To send a file from one, usually smaller, computer to a server or host.

**URL:** "Uniform Resource Locator." The "address" or "location" of a website. URLs are in the form hostname.domain — for example, **bedfordstmartins .com** — and usually are preceded by **http://**.

**Username:** A pseudonym used to login (or log on) to a website; also called "login name." See "Login."

**Website:** A virtual place on the World Wide Web that contains multimedia and text. All websites have a URL that web browsers can use to locate them.

**WWW:** "World Wide Web." A medium on the Internet used for multimedia and interactive electronic communication using web browsers such as Internet Explorer, Opera, or Netscape.

# Primary Source Index

References are to the website entry numbers.

Advertising, 15, 23, 96, 147, 160, 167, 172, 180, 236, 238

Artifacts and Objects, 14, 31, 43, 97, 105, 109, 175

Film and Video, 2, 4, 136, 138, 154, 162, 169, 210, 214, 232, 238, 247, 249

Letters and Diaries, 2, 4, 14, 15, 40, 50, 58, 62, 65, 79, 104, 107, 115, 129, 207

Literary Sources, 2, 4, 14, 17, 31, 34, 59, 68, 69, 73, 77, 81, 88, 98, 100, 102, 111, 113, 115, 124, 128, 138, 139, 148, 153, 155, 176, 197, 216

Maps, 1, 4, 6, 29, 39, 52, 57, 60, 91, 101, 112, 212

Music, 4, 15, 34, 64, 78, 134, 144, 149, 154, 162, 165, 188, 193, 198, 201, 203, 215

Newspapers and Periodicals, 13, 14, 18, 19, 20, 26, 27, 33, 41, 52, 65, 66, 73, 75, 95, 96, 98, 101, 111, 114, 117, 118, 124, 131, 132, 133, 135, 153, 157, 158, 159, 160, 163, 166, 170, 173, 174, 180, 182, 196, 205, 226, 233, 234, 249

Official Documents, 3, 4, 6, 7, 8, 13, 14, 16, 18, 24, 25, 27, 28, 35, 36, 38, 44, 45, 46, 47, 48, 49, 51, 53, 54, 56, 58, 61, 62, 64, 65, 67, 71, 72, 85, 93, 94, 101, 105, 109, 116, 125, 132, 143, 149, 151, 164, 179, 192, 194, 206, 209, 211, 220, 222, 227, 228, 230, 231, 235, 237, 241, 242, 244, 245, 249

Oral History, 2, 4, 21, 26, 28, 32, 74, 115, 123, 135, 156, 174, 181, 184, 186, 189, 191, 199, 200, 202, 207, 208, 210, 217, 220, 222, 223, 224, 225, 232, 239, 240, 243, 250

Paintings and Prints, 14, 17, 37, 39, 59, 60, 92, 95, 107, 113, 116, 121, 122, 126, 134, 166, 187, 195, 234

Personal Accounts, 2, 9, 15, 31, 34, 36, 40, 45, 46, 50, 52, 53, 55, 58, 61, 62, 65, 68, 71, 73, 79, 81, 82, 87, 88, 89, 90, 92, 93, 101, 106, 107, 109, 115, 117, 122, 128, 129, 133, 141, 149, 158, 161, 164, 173, 179, 184, 196, 218, 229, 247

Photographs, 4, 6, 8, 10, 12, 14, 15, 17, 26, 31, 32, 34, 36, 70, 76, 90, 91, 92, 99, 105, 106, 108, 114, 116, 119, 120, 121, 126, 127, 129, 130, 133, 140, 141, 143, 146, 150, 161, 162, 163, 164, 167, 168, 171, 174, 175, 177, 178, 179, 183, 185, 189, 192, 194, 195, 196, 197, 199, 201, 207, 217, 247, 250

Political Cartoons, 14, 118, 139, 142, 170, 190, 234

Political Documents, 3, 5, 22, 24, 36, 47, 58, 61, 62, 63, 64, 65, 80, 83, 85, 89, 131, 139, 148, 149, 152, 156, 158, 159, 176, 182, 196, 204, 207, 216, 217, 218, 219, 221, 222, 223, 232, 234, 237, 238, 248, 250

Quantitative Evidence, 16, 28, 35, 46, 84, 101, 219, 227, 228, 230, 235, 246

Religious Texts, 26, 45, 47, 86, 103, 115

Sheet Music, 4, 15, 78, 134, 162

Speeches, 3, 9, 13, 24, 61, 64, 89, 103, 106, 137, 139, 145, 149, 152, 155, 176, 196, 213, 218, 221, 222

# Subject Index

References are to the website entry numbers.

Abolitionism, 1, 4, 7, 9, 36, 58, 72, 74, 81, 85, 100, 101, 133

Addams, Jane, 173

African Americans, 1, 2, 4, 6, 15, 17, 28, 34, 36, 55, 64, 66, 67, 68, 78, 94, 100, 103, 106, 115, 120, 133, 134, 153, 158, 165, 167, 178, 188, 196, 198, 199, 201, 202, 204, 205, 207, 215, 218, 221, 228, 231

AIDS (Acquired Immune Deficiency Syndrome)/HIV (Human Immunodeficiency Virus), 32, 226

Alabama, 13, 43

American Indians, 6, 7, 13, 14, 17, 25, 39, 42, 43, 44, 52, 56, 71, 79, 105, 107, 119, 121, 122, 125, 126, 127, 146, 150, 164, 167, 171, 204, 228, 239

American Revolution, 9, 29, 48, 49, 51, 53, 54, 58, 61, 62, 63

*Amistad,* 18, 85

Anarchism, 18, 36, 109, 148, 152, 156, 204, 206

Anticommunism, 109, 204, 206, 208, 216

Architecture, 8, 12, 174

Art, 37, 39, 76, 162, 186, 187

Asian Americans, 2, 32, 91, 95, 141, 143, 161, 174, 185, 189, 204, 222, 228

Bell, Alexander Graham, 104

Birth Control, 159, 204

Black Panthers, 204, 231

Brown, John, 85, 97, 101

Bryan, William Jennings, 145, 152

Business, 27, 123, 130, 132, 147, 160, 175, 191, 214, 227, 230, 236, 240, 243

California, 32, 107, 125, 141, 161, 203

Carter, Jimmy, 14

Catt, Carrie Chapman, 176

Central Intelligence Agency (CIA), 242

Chicago, 18, 109, 117, 163, 173, 202

Chinese Americans, 91, 95, 141, 161, 174

Cities, 8, 9, 12, 15, 29, 107, 117, 126, 153, 157, 161, 163, 171, 173, 174, 177, 195, 215, 228, 233

Civil Rights, 189, 207, 217, 218, 231

Civil War, 1, 2, 15, 29, 34, 66, 92, 95, 96, 99, 101, 115

Clinton, William Jefferson, 205, 245

Coal Mining, 26, 28, 110

Cold War, 7, 152, 204, 206, 209, 211, 214, 220

Colorado, 119, 193

Communism, 18, 156, 182, 204, 208, 209, 216, 231

Computers, 34, 240

Confederate States of America, 7, 48, 92, 93

Congress, 16, 48, 49, 116, 125

Connecticut, 10, 38, 130

Consumer Culture, 15, 23, 75, 95, 97, 113, 118, 124, 147, 160, 167, 180, 214, 227, 230, 236, 238, 240

Continental Congress, 48, 49

Coolidge, Calvin, 137, 152

Cuba, 206, 209, 211

Declaration of Independence, 51, 54, 80

Depression, 26, 28, 90, 183, 184, 186, 187, 189, 190, 192, 195, 196, 197, 199, 202, 203, 208

Desegregation, 205, 207, 222

Disabilities, 114

Douglass, Frederick, 47, 83, 103

Du Bois, W. E. B., 47, 152

Dust Bowl, 183, 203

Economy, 11, 19, 35, 111, 227, 228, 230, 235, 250

Edison, Thomas A., 132, 145, 154

Education, 5, 11, 17, 21, 35, 61, 86, 88, 104, 122, 136, 167, 200, 205, 214

Eisenhower, Dwight D., 205

Elections, 16, 95, 219, 238

Emerson, Ralph Waldo, 47, 69

Environment and Conservation, 10, 57, 107, 116, 119, 128, 150, 164, 241, 250

Ethnicity, 10, 35, 78, 156, 173, 175, 243

Exploration, 46, 52, 57, 60, 79

Family Life, 10, 13, 36, 44, 86, 88, 94, 120, 129, 140, 184, 210

Florida, 150, 164

Folk Music, 193, 198, 201

Freedmen's Bureau, 94, 101

Garrison, William Lloyd, 83, 85

Garvey, Marcus, 158

Georgia, 14, 198

Gold Rush, 107, 161

Goldman, Emma, 148, 152, 156, 204

Gompers, Samuel, 137, 145

Gulf War, 232

Harlem, 126, 153

Hawaii, 143, 237, 239

Health and Medicine, 5, 17, 27, 36, 50, 92, 114,
116, 160, 179, 214, 226, 235, 236, 246
Hughes, Langston, 153
Hull House, 173

Ideologies, Political and Religious, 11, 47, 49,
51, 54, 59, 61, 62, 63, 69, 73, 80, 106, 139,
148, 153, 158, 182, 208, 213, 218
Immigration, 2, 35, 46, 52, 57, 128, 140, 141,
142, 157, 161, 173, 189
Imperialism, 139, 166, 237
International Relations, 3, 7, 29, 58, 95, 139,
143, 149, 151, 166, 169, 179, 192, 206, 209,
211, 212, 217, 220, 221, 222, 224, 228, 232,
237, 241, 242, 245, 250

Japanese Americans, internment of, 32, 161,
185, 189, 222
Jay, John, 58
Jazz, 126, 165, 188, 215
Jefferson, Thomas, 28, 51, 55, 61, 62
Jews, 32, 57, 150, 156
Johnson, Andrew, 18, 48, 95
Johnson, Lyndon B., 213, 217
Journalism, 22, 73, 75, 95, 96, 117, 131, 163,
170, 205, 225, 233, 234, 249

Kennedy, John F., 211, 213
Kennedy, Robert F., 221
Kentucky, 26
King, Martin Luther, Jr., 152, 213, 218
Korean Americans, 174
Ku Klux Klan, 142, 204, 231

Labor and Labor Movements, 10, 26, 28, 36, 80,
94, 110, 119, 120, 123, 136, 140, 167, 175,
182, 184, 191, 196, 202, 208, 230, 233, 246
Latinos, 2, 13, 168, 174, 193, 228
Legal History, 3, 6, 7, 14, 18, 24, 25, 27, 32, 38,
44, 45, 48, 49, 56, 58, 64, 65, 72, 85, 101,
109, 143, 159, 189, 231, 235, 237, 241, 244,
245
Lewis and Clark Expedition, 60, 79
Lincoln, Abraham, 64, 65, 97
Literature, 2, 17, 19, 34, 39, 68, 69, 73, 75, 77,
81, 98, 100, 102, 115, 118, 124, 153, 155,
216
Little Rock, Arkansas, 205
London, Jack, 155
Louisiana, 48, 199

Maine, 50, 57
Michigan, 128, 191
Mid-Atlantic States, 9, 56, 58, 66, 67, 70, 73, 74,
92, 96, 97, 98, 101, 104, 108, 112, 126, 130,
157, 195, 233

Midwestern States, 26, 31, 52, 64, 72, 109, 112,
128, 129, 133, 163, 172, 173, 175, 177, 191,
243
Migration, 52, 87, 127, 129
Military History, 2, 3, 6, 14, 15, 28, 29, 34, 53,
65, 66, 92, 96, 99, 101, 118, 143, 149, 166,
168, 169, 170, 179, 181, 192, 194, 200, 202,
206, 210, 211, 217, 220, 224, 232, 241, 242,
243
Mississippi, 207, 231
Mormons, 47, 86, 87
Motion Pictures, 13, 132, 136, 154, 162, 169, 214

Nast, Thomas, 95, 118
National Parks, 8, 29, 164
Nativism, 137, 141, 142
Nebraska, 129
New Deal, 26, 28, 183, 184, 186, 187, 196, 197,
202
New England, 10, 12, 38, 44, 45, 50, 57, 69, 89,
112
New Jersey, 66, 130, 132, 200
New York, 56, 58, 77, 92, 96, 97, 98, 126, 130,
140, 157, 195, 226, 233
Nixon, Richard M., 213, 249
North Atlantic Treaty Organization (NATO),
211, 220, 222
North Carolina, 115

Office of War Information, 183, 195
Ohio, 31, 52, 131, 133, 142, 243
Oregon, 82, 125

Paine, Thomas, 63
Pearl Harbor, 181
Pennsylvania, 66, 67, 74, 101
Philippines, 15, 166
Photography, 70, 76, 99, 130
Poe, Edgar Allan, 17, 73
Politics, 3, 4, 7, 11, 16, 19, 24, 27, 36, 38, 40, 48,
49, 51, 53, 58, 59, 61, 62, 64, 65, 95, 96,
118, 133, 137, 139, 145, 149, 150, 152, 176,
179, 190, 192, 196, 212, 213, 217, 219, 222,
223, 234, 235, 237, 238, 245, 249
Popular Culture, 2, 4, 5, 15, 34, 75, 76, 78, 95,
97, 98, 100, 108, 113, 117, 118, 124, 126,
134, 135, 136, 138, 144, 154, 162, 165, 172,
177, 180, 188, 190, 193, 195, 198, 201, 203,
215, 216
Population, 29, 35, 212, 228, 230
Progressive Era, 36, 106, 110, 131, 140, 157,
173, 176
Prohibition, 131, 142

Radicalism, 32, 63, 109, 145, 148, 152, 155, 158,
182, 204, 208, 216, 231, 233, 250

Railroads, 29, 60, 91
Reform, 1, 69, 80, 83, 89, 103, 114, 125, 131,
    142, 152, 156, 157, 159, 173, 176, 207, 218,
    248
Religion, 12, 28, 39, 45, 47, 59, 86, 87, 88, 98,
    103, 115, 122, 129, 133, 142, 156, 193, 218,
    246
Roosevelt, Franklin D., 114, 137, 152, 190, 192,
    196
Rosenberg, Julius and Ethel, 18, 204, 206
Rural Life, 8, 26, 110, 111, 123, 129, 130, 168,
    177, 183, 184, 196, 203

Sacco and Vanzetti, 18, 204, 231
Salem Witch Trials, 18, 45
San Francisco, California, 141, 161
Sanger, Margaret, 159
Science and Technology, 4, 8, 19, 34, 70, 76, 91,
    98, 104, 108, 111, 126, 132, 154, 214, 229,
    232, 240
Scopes Trial, 18, 142
Scott, Dred, 72
Scottsboro Boys, 18, 204
September 11, 2001, 7, 195, 242, 247
Sexuality, 36, 159, 226, 231
Slavery, 1, 5, 7, 13, 37, 40, 41, 52, 55, 58, 67, 72,
    74, 81, 83, 84, 85, 90, 93, 100, 103, 115,
    120, 184
Southern States, 1, 9, 14, 26, 28, 37, 40, 41, 43,
    46, 48, 55, 62, 71, 81, 90, 92, 93, 94, 101,
    106, 112, 115, 123, 150, 164, 168, 183, 198,
    199, 201, 205, 207
Spanish-American War, 126, 139, 166, 169,
    171
Sports, 135, 163
Stowe, Harriet Beecher, 47, 100
Strikes, 110, 123, 191

Suffrage, Woman, 32, 176

Television, 180, 238
Terkel, Studs, 202
Texas, 168
Textile Industry, 10, 123
Theater, 2, 134, 162, 197
Tobacco, 95, 147, 236
Transcendentalism, 69
Truman, Harry S., 222
Twain, Mark, 124, 139, 166

Underground Railroad, 67, 74, 81
United Nations, 192, 222

Vesey, Denmark, 85
Veterans, 210
Vietnam War, 210, 217, 224, 233
Virginia, 28, 40, 41, 46, 60, 61, 62, 84, 101

Washington, Booker T., 103, 106, 145
Washington, D.C., 9, 85, 99, 104
Washington, George, 29, 47, 51, 53, 58
Watergate, 231, 234, 249
Western States, 32, 60, 71, 79, 82, 87, 91, 105,
    107, 112, 116, 119, 121, 122, 125, 126, 127,
    141, 146, 161, 171, 174, 183, 185, 189, 193,
    203, 208, 237, 240
Westward Expansion, 60, 71, 79, 82, 87, 107,
    119, 125, 126, 127
Wisconsin, 128, 177
Women, 2, 5, 15, 23, 32, 36, 44, 45, 50, 64, 66,
    68, 75, 78, 80, 88, 89, 131, 142, 148, 156,
    159, 167, 173, 176, 225, 228, 246, 248
Women's Rights, 15, 24, 36, 89, 176, 216, 248
World War I, 7, 115, 149, 167, 170, 179, 210
World War II, 7, 181, 194, 200, 202, 210